HE'LL
BE
OK

HE'LL BE OK

GROWING GORGEOUS BOYS INTO GOOD MEN

Celia Lashlie

 HarperCollins*Publishers*

National Library of Australia Cataloguing-in-Publication Data

Lashlie, Celia.
He'll be OK : growing gorgeous boys into good men.
Australian ed.
ISBN 13: 978 0 7322 8450 3
ISBN 10: 0 7322 8450 3
1. Teenage boys – Psychology. 2. Teenage boys – Conduct of
life. 3. Parent and teenager. 4. Child rearing. I. Title.
649.132

First published 2005
This edition published 2007
Reprinted 2007 (ten times), 2008 (four times), 2009, 2010 (twice)
HarperCollins*Publishers (New Zealand) Limited*
P.O. Box 1, Auckland

10-digit ISBN 0 7322 8450 3
13-digit ISBN 978 0 7322 8450 3

Cover design by Darren Holt, HarperCollins Design Studio
Typesetting by Janine Brougham

Printed by Griffin Press, Australia

70gsm Classic used by HarperCollins*Publishers* is a natural, recyclable product
made from wood grown in sustainable forests. The manufacturing processes
conform to the environmental regulations in the country of origin, Finland.

For the many good men I met on the journey:
know how special you are.

For the many gorgeous boys I met on the journey:
know that magic lies within you.

For Bek and Gene
and all who continue to walk with me
on the journey of life:
know it is you who give my life meaning.

Contents

Foreword

Recently I was invited to convene a breakfast given for fathers whose sons attended a Gosford grammar school. Most of these fathers commuted at least 50 kilometres to Sydney to work, which meant they left before their sons had breakfasted and returned in the evening as they were settling down to homework. A number of fathers had spoken to the school principal of their concern that their boys were growing up without them.

Wisely, the school recognised the need for these fathers to be involved in their boys' daily life. As most of the fathers had never met each other either, the school wanted to bring them together and see if there was common ground. Was it just lack of time spent together, a lack of communication? Or were the fathers more committed to their work than to their sons?

I spoke first of my 25 years of experience as a lawyer representing children and then sitting as a magistrate in the Children's Court. After that I threw the meeting open for discussion. I invited the men present to ask me any questions they liked. They could ask about my court work, or about what it was like to be a woman confronting men who, in my view, weren't worth a bootlace in the father stakes. Or they could just talk about how they felt about fatherhood.

At first it was like pulling teeth. One hand went up, then slowly another. But as soon as the first father spoke about the biggest problem he faced — how to communicate with his son — the floodgates opened. Nobody worried any more about putting his hand up. They all spoke to each other, nodding in agreement as they realised they shared the same fears and worries. And then one father took over, saying that if they all felt the same, perhaps they could also work out solutions together.

Telephone numbers were exchanged; they spoke of going to sports fixtures together rather than in separate cars; they spoke of travelling to Sydney in a group. They exchanged suggestions: perhaps the boys could do their homework before dinner so that the family could sit down to a meal together; maybe the TV could be turned off. I knew the breakfast had been a success when, as I was leaving, I heard a group organising a camping weekend with their sons — no women allowed.

That day taught me something which is outlined in Celia Lashlie's book. How do you learn about the way boys — and men — think, or the way they act as they do? You ask them. This is where Lashlie's prior experience working with men in prisons has stood her in good stead. In *He'll Be OK* boy after boy reveals previously unspoken truths. They show that boys go straight to the chase, aren't sidetracked by what they see as trifling issues, don't have time to dwell on things.

This is a book about how boys verbalise — or don't; how they express anger — or don't. And, radically, it's a book about the father-son relationship. It is not an anti-mothers book; it simply acknowledges the importance of the interaction between dads and their boys. We're becoming more and more aware of the importance of this bond as a boy seeks a hero, an idol, someone who understands what it is to be a male. And who better for this role than his father.

I used to believe that if we could bottle the strength of male adolescent peer pressure, we could send a man to the moon, but Celia Lashlie contends that it is boys' sense of loyalty which is strong; so strong that they will stand shoulder to shoulder rather than let a mate down, no matter how crazy the idea. After reading this book, I now think she is right — loyalty is a major force driving boys.

Not everyone, perhaps, will agree with Celia Lashlie's findings, but this is a book which will remain with you long after you've read it. Her commitment to accurate research is evident in the conclusions and advice she sets out for us to read and digest. I know I've added a valuable reference book to my library, one which convinces me that boys are not as mysterious as some would have us believe, that there are reasons behind their actions, that they can grow into good men. How do I know this? Because Celia told me so.

Barbara Holborow
Sydney, 2006

Introduction:
The Beginning of the Journey

A few months ago, while I was still considering whether there was any real merit in writing a book about what I'd learnt as a result of my participation in the Good Man Project, I sat in a café and watched the interaction between a man and his three young sons, aged between four and eight. As I unashamedly eavesdropped on their conversation, it became apparent that the boys' mother had passed responsibility to Dad for the morning.

What drew my attention was the very calm approach of the father as he dealt with three extremely energetic boys. He allowed them time to clamber up onto the seats they'd selected and spoke clearly and slowly to them about what they might like to eat and drink. He gave them plenty of time to make their choices and didn't appear to get at all agitated when, more than once, they became distracted by something else in the busy café. When the youngest boy got down off his chair to investigate something he'd seen on the floor, his father just quietly asked him to sit down again, which the child did in his own time; no harm was done in the meantime.

When the food arrived, the father helped where necessary,

but generally left the boys to manage it themselves and didn't become upset when, as was inevitable, things got a bit messy. He let them wander from the table once they'd finished eating, never rushing to stop them doing whatever they were focused on, but always keeping an eye on them and pulling them back within his reach whenever he deemed it necessary. The boys seemed to relax into their father's calmness, knowing intuitively how far they could go before he would call them back. His voice was their boundary: he knew it and so did the boys. As I watched, I couldn't help but wonder just how different things might have been if the boys had been in the company of their mother or another woman.

A week or two later I boarded a plane and found myself sitting across the aisle from a man and his son, a boy of about ten. The boy's mother and the younger brother, aged about four, were seated behind me.

The father and son were talking in low tones about the plane and what was happening outside on the tarmac, and as we prepared to take off, I noticed the father reach for his son's hand and cradle it within his, presumably to reassure him. Once the plane was in the air, a commentary from the seat behind me began as the mother checked continually on the wellbeing of her elder son. At least every two or three minutes, or so it seemed, she asked the father whether the boy was 'all right', while at the same time working to keep an energetic four-year-old under control.

Perhaps I'm being a bit hard on the woman, but she appeared to be undermining the father's attempts to relate positively and reassuringly to his son. Having made several enquiries and comments about the boy's welfare, she then went on to contradict her husband. When he asked the flight attendant for coffee, from across the aisle (and one seat back!), she said, 'But wouldn't you prefer tea?' She seemed to have decided that she needed to be involved in everything that was happening with both her sons, while at the same time trying to manage what their father was choosing to drink.

In a way, the comparison between these two incidents has pushed me to write this book. I consider myself a feminist: I see feminism as the right of women to pursue whatever path they choose without in any way being restricted by their gender. My chosen direction in life has been strongly influenced by a desire to be free, while working to ensure that same freedom for everyone with whom I come in contact. I consider it extremely important that my freedom not come at the cost of anyone else's. Unfortunately, my experience within the Good Man Project has left me with the impression that women's quest for freedom has perhaps taken its toll on our perception of men and manhood.

> 'I lost my jacket in the pavilion yesterday. If anyone picked it up I'd be grateful to have it back. Of course my wife says it isn't lost until she's had a look for it.'

In August 2002 I published *The Journey to Prison: Who Goes and Why*, a book I was persuaded to write because of a growing interest, within various communities, in imprisonment and the issues associated with it. The opinions about crime and punishment I'd heard being expressed over a number of years in the media and in general conversation often seemed short on facts and I considered there might be value in sharing some of what I'd discovered while working inside the world of prisons.

Since writing that first book, I've been on another journey, one that has taken me away from the world of prisons and into the world of boys' schools, one that has allowed me to revel fully in the delight that is adolescent boys. The journey has involved working in a number of New Zealand boys' schools on the Good Man Project, which was undertaken in the hope it would facilitate discussion within and between boys' schools about what makes a good man in the 21st century.

It was intended to be a small piece of work that would involve 'just a few' boys' schools and take 'just a few' months, but the project grew and in the 18 months between September 2002 and March 2004 I worked in 25 boys' schools across New Zealand. It was an amazing experience, one that taught me a great deal both about myself and about adolescent boys and the world they occupy. It proved to be a wonderful contrast to the time I'd spent in prison wings where I'd often grieved for the lost potential of the young men I was meeting.

During the Good Man Project, discussions about the concept of contemporary manhood flourished among teachers, parents and the students themselves, and it began to seem that this was an idea whose time had come.

When the project was being mooted, I was looking through the eyes of a woman who, in her role as the single parent of two children, had coped reasonably well with her daughter's sometimes rough journey through adolescence, but who had regularly lost her way when accompanying her son on the same journey. With that experience still very much alive in my mind, I was keen to be involved for both personal and professional reasons.

Following my visits to the 25 schools, I completed a report

to the principals that summarised my findings, identifying what their schools do really well in their quest to educate young men, and setting out some ideas about what they might do better. Their response to the report has been extremely positive and a number of initiatives under way within the schools are a direct result of their involvement in the project.

What neither the principals nor I anticipated was the level of interest that would be shown in the project and its findings by the parents, both mothers and fathers, of the students involved. In the course of each school visit, it became usual practice to invite parents to a meeting to hear about the project, including the process being followed and why the school was spending money in this way. Attendances were always good, in some cases significantly beyond what had been hoped for. What I was saying about their sons struck a real chord with the parents: laughter and many 'aha' moments were a regular feature of the discussions.

And so I've agreed to write a second book, in order to bring the findings of the project and the stories of the students out into the wider community, and to explore a little further how we might all work together more effectively to keep young men safe as they ride the roller-coaster that is male adolescence.

I've also written the book to honour men, their skill, their intuition, their pragmatism and their humour and their extraordinary ability to become boys again at a moment's notice, whatever their age. I also want to suggest to women, in particular mothers, that, consciously or unconsciously, they're preventing men from using their talents in raising their boys. The answer to the things that worry us most about our boys lies in recognising who they are rather than in trying to make them who they're not.

We seem to lose far too many of our young men to suicide, to prison and to horrific deaths on the roads. A significant number of those in prison will be young men — young men with enormous potential who have made stupid decisions as part of their quest for manhood. These decisions have taken them to the prison gates and created pain and suffering for numerous others, including their victims and their own families.

'How is it, do you think, that young men like you sometimes get into so much trouble?'

'Some nights are really boring and you just want to go out and create some carnage. You don't think of the consequences at the beginning, but you do once you're in the middle of the act and usually that's too late.'

As I think about the lost potential of those killed on the roads and the way in which their families will have been ripped apart, I'm moved yet again to wonder what we have to do to prevent such loss in the future. I can only hope that this book may add to the discussion already occurring within families and communities about how to reduce the negative statistics and enable more of our gorgeous boys to grow into good men.

I'm able to write this book because of the graciousness of the principals who, having shown remarkable insight by becoming involved in the project in the first place, have been willing to share with a larger audience information that rightly belongs to their schools.

Above all else, I've written this book in an attempt to share the magic I encountered inside the world of boys' schools and inside the minds of adolescent boys. They're gorgeous creatures, full of potential. They may drive us to distraction as they hurtle recklessly towards adulthood, then decide they want to remain boys for just a little longer and turn back to play, and we may often wonder whether they, and we, will make it to their 20th birthday. But they're also insightful individuals who carry in their heads the answers to many of the questions we have about them and who can show us the way forward if we will only pause long enough to ask the question . . . and then wait graciously (and silently) for the answer.

Chapter 1
What Was the Good Man Project?

The Good Man Project grew out of an energetic discussion that took place at a Heads of Boys' Schools Conference hosted by Nelson College, an innovative and respected private New Zealand boys' high school, in September 2001. The talk had focused on such questions as 'What is the definition of a good man?', 'What is the essence of being male?' and 'What does it mean to be a young man in today's world?'

As I've mentioned, the aim of the project was to develop a working definition of what makes a good man in the 21st century, a definition it was hoped would influence the schools' education of their students.

After working in male prisons for a number of years I'd concluded that, for many young men, prison becomes a rite of passage, the place where they end up as a result of their misguided attempts to prove to the adults around them, and to themselves, that they're men. They don't go to prison deliberately; rather, they go almost accidentally, having chosen to indulge in behaviour they see as manly without pausing to consider the likely consequences. That behaviour includes drinking alcohol in significant quantities, fighting to defend their own or their mates' honour and driving cars too fast.

After 15 years in the New Zealand prison system, I began to work a little more closely with at-risk adolescents and became increasingly interested in investigating the rites of passage that might be used to stem the flow of young men into our prisons. One project I became involved in took me into Nelson College. As I wandered the halls for the first time I wondered how a traditional boys' school like this managed its at-risk students. As such boys became problematic, did they just move them down the road to the local co-ed, turn their backs on them and concentrate on those students whose progress reflected well on the school? Or did they make genuine attempts to meet the needs of these students even when the going got tough?

In the course of the regular visits I was making to the school, I began to debate this issue with the principal, Salvi Gargiulo, who, it was easy to see, was passionate about boys and their education. During one of our conversations I talked about prison, linking it to male rites of passage. I could practically see Salvi's brain stretching as I put the words 'Nelson College' and 'prison' into the same sentence. His response to the idea that there could be any connection between the two things was to comment on the long and esteemed history of the school. My immediate response was that, long history notwithstanding, I had met a number of the school's old boys in my previous life. That focused the conversation a little, and we continued to talk and laugh.

At one stage in the discussion, I found myself talking about how silent, in my view, men had become: we don't seem to hear their voices in debates about boys and manhood as much as we used to. Salvi's response: 'We really need a men's revolution, don't we?' I looked back at him and said, 'Yeah, you do.' Then he did a very bloke-ish thing: he grinned at me and said, 'I don't suppose we could get you to do it for us?' The women reading this will understand that as a typical male response in those circumstances, that is, something needs doing and if I wait long enough and apply a little psychological pressure, she just might do it for me.

My response to the suggestion that I lead a male revolution was an immediate no, something that seemed to surprise Salvi. I then made the point that it was a men's revolution we were talking about. 'I'm a woman — we women have had our revolution and we won. We're actually running the country now.' Completely unfazed by this slight glitch in his plan, he then looked at me and said, 'Well, if you won't run the revolution, will you at least come to the Heads of Boys' Schools Conference I'm hosting?'

This question drew a second no from me. 'They'll be stuffy, boring old farts. They'll only want to talk about rugby and I've had enough time in the prison service to have done my dash in terms of talking about rugby. And anyway, they won't be interested in anything I have to say. From the moment I walk in, they'll have me classified as a radical feminist lesbian and that will be that.' The look on Salvi's face at that point suggested he was wondering exactly which part of any such classification might be wrong. After a bit more discussion on the topic, Salvi persuaded me there would be merit in meeting his colleagues so I agreed to spend an hour with them.

I went for an hour, I stayed for the day and I had a great time. They didn't want to talk only about rugby and they didn't appear to classify me as a radical feminist lesbian — well, not that I could detect anyway. Nor were they stuffy, boring old farts. They were intelligent, articulate men with a clearly discernible interest in and passion for boys' education. They demonstrated highly developed senses of humour and showed themselves well able to debate new and challenging ideas.

In the course of the discussion with the 14 principals present at that September 2001 meeting, I drew a link between the world of boys' schools and the world of prisons and challenged those present to lead the debate today's society must have about manhood in the 21st century. What does manhood involve? How does a boy become a man? What role do/should men such as themselves, in positions of leadership within a male environment, play in bringing boys across the bridge of adolescence?

It seemed to me that the principals were (and continue to be) very well placed to identify and provide more positive rites of passage, rites of passage that celebrate manhood and maleness rather than denigrating it, while increasing the chances of young men making it safely into adulthood.

During the discussion of the concept of manhood in today's world, someone in the group said the words 'good man'. Straight away I asked what the definition of a good man was and in that moment I received my first lesson about the real difference between the genders: 14 men sat looking at one another around the table in complete silence. Being a woman, I naturally assumed that the silence meant they didn't know the answer to the question. After all, if I'd asked 14 women for the definition of a good woman, I'm reasonably confident the answers would have begun almost immediately and a vigorous debate would have followed. But it wasn't that the men didn't know the answer to the question; they were silent because they were thinking.

The basic difference between men and women? Forget biology and whatever else you might think constitutes the major difference between the genders. I learned in that moment, and continued to learn throughout the project, that the foremost difference between men and women is that we women think and talk at the same time. We learn what we think about something by talking about it. We start in one place on an issue, keep talking it through with someone, usually another woman, and often end up in a completely different place (with the men in our lives frequently lamenting silently that we're continually changing our minds). In fact we aren't changing our minds: we're simply establishing what we think — out loud. Men, on the other hand, think, then talk and there's often a gap, sometimes an enormous gap, between the two processes. In terms of effective inter-gender communication, this is often where the problem starts. We women sense the existence of the gap and immediately move to fill it in by talking to the man and interrupting his thinking processes.

This isn't about intelligence. Don't be tempted to take offence because I'm suggesting one gender is naturally more intelligent than the other. This is all about process. We just think differently.

So there was a long pause, and then all of a sudden the conversation took off and they were away. 'Wouldn't it be great to have a definition of a good man? What do you think might be in there?' The debate raged. As a woman, I was somewhat nonplussed that there wasn't already a definition they could immediately call on and I said so. 'Hey guys, thousands of women all over the country are giving you their boys in the hope you'll help raise them to manhood and turn them into good men and you've got no bloody idea what you're doing.' 'Oh no, no,' they replied, 'we've got *some* idea.' I have to say I wasn't reassured.

Salvi recognised the value of the conversation and as the day drew to a close, those present agreed that I would return in the not too distant future to continue talking with him about this topic to see what, if anything, might be done to take the idea further. And so the Good Man Project was born. In subsequent discussions we agreed there was a conversation to be had and that it was worthwhile exploring further the idea of manhood and rites of passage within the laboratory that is boys' schools. How that conversation might take place was something we trusted would unfold in time. All we had to do was to work out the first steps to be taken and the rest would follow. And so it proved.

The plan was that all boys' secondary schools in New Zealand would be invited to take part in what we were classifying as loose (very loose) action research. I would spend three days at each school that wished to take part in the project, this being seen as a reasonable amount of time in which to immerse myself in the culture of the school. I would then see where the discussions about manhood led me. Initially six schools were willing to take a risk with this idea (and willing to try to find some funding) and it was with their backing the project got under way. My first visit took place in September 2002.

As the visits to the first half-dozen schools continued across the fourth term of that year and word about the project began to spread, another eight schools enrolled. Then, following a presentation about the project and some of the preliminary findings to a conference organised by the newly formed Association of Boys' Schools in April

2003, another ten schools enrolled. The final number of participating schools was 25. This included 18 state-funded, four integrated and three private schools. (Integrated schools are generally religious schools that used to operate privately but have been integrated into the state system and receive government funding. Although they follow the state curriculum requirements, they retain their special religious or philosophical character.)

The project involved no government funding. The principals and I agreed that we would operate outside the bureaucracy because that would mean fewer boundaries and no red tape. We wouldn't need to concern ourselves with political correctness and we could follow whatever leads presented themselves in terms of gaining admission to the world of adolescent boys. My only concern in terms of how I worked was to ensure I was on side with the school principals as they were in effect my employers. The complete absence of bureaucracy meant there were no restrictions on what I could discuss with the boys, a freedom I came to appreciate and value.

Each of the schools taking part did so on the understanding that they would have to find the necessary funds within their already stretched budgets. This I thought extraordinary: it showed their commitment to their students and their staff, and their belief that everyone within their school community would benefit from being involved.

Scheduling the visits proved to be a major task as I tried to fit in with school calendars. There was a great deal of travel up and down the country. The fee each school would pay to participate in the project was agreed at the outset and included a travel component that allowed the equalisation of project expenses across all participating schools. To minimise costs, where possible I combined a school visit with a speaking engagement that had been scheduled in the same area, and I relied heavily on friends for accommodation. This was a project undertaken with a great deal of enthusiasm and very limited financial resources.

The 25 schools that took part in the project were spread throughout the country and covered a range of socio-economic groups. Twelve had started life as co-educational institutions, and then separated into single-sex boys' and girls' schools at a later date, mostly because their sites were too small for their growing school populations.

Only one co-educational school took part in the project and it did so because the school management team considered there would be definite value in assessing the impact of bringing girls into a school that had been a boys' institution for all but the last 13 years of its 150-year history.

The project was never about whether boys' schools are 'better' for boys than co-educational schools. Rather it was about identifying the points of difference within boys' schools, including what they do well. It was hoped this information would then help parents to decide whether a co-educational school or a single-sex school might best suit their son.

The project meant we could explore ideas about manhood in an all-male environment without having to pause and ask, 'What about the girls?' There are and always will be boys who'll do well in an all-male environment while others will flourish in a co-educational setting. It's entirely possible that two boys from one family could suit the two different types of school available to them.

As I've said, each school visit lasted three days. During that time, I held conversations with staff and management and with as wide and diverse a range of students as possible. On the first morning of each visit I explained the reasons behind the project to staff at their morning briefing and invited those who wanted to share their views on boys' education, male rites of passage and/or associated issues to discuss their ideas with me in either a group or a one-to-one setting at some point over the following three days. This invitation always brought an immediate and very positive response.

On some occasions I finished my introduction of the project by challenging the male teachers in the room to think about when they'd become men. The silence was often deafening until they realised I didn't want them to disclose the information then and there, but just to think about it and perhaps, once they'd worked out the answer to the question, to share it with their sons, their male colleagues and maybe even their partners.

After making it clear that I wanted access to the widest possible range of students, in terms of age and academic ability, I left it to the school to select which classes I should talk to. Having heard about the project at the staff briefing, many teachers immediately volunteered their classes, some no doubt so they could take the opportunity to attend to other more pressing matters, but most because they believed their particular class would provide some interesting insights into the world of adolescent boys. At no point did I struggle to get access to sufficient numbers of students: quite the reverse in fact. There was an endless number of willing participants, access to them limited only by my durability and energy levels.

The conversations with individual staff usually started with me asking 'Why are you working/teaching in a boys' school?' and led on to discussion of a wide range of issues associated with boys and their education. In the course of the project I talked with approximately 110 individual staff members and took part in a number of delightfully energetic group discussions in various school staffrooms.

I was impressed by the degree of enthusiasm staff had for their work, and for boys' education in general, and by their willingness to be exposed to, and openly discuss, new ideas. Many of these discussions had us all in fits of laughter as we explored the reality of working in the presence of large numbers of adolescent boys.

I was often amused and entertained by the men present in the staffrooms, their humour, their quick wit and the way in which they communicated non-verbally but very clearly and succinctly with one another. As the men revelled in being in each other's company, I noted that insults were regularly traded, one-liners were the norm and laughter abounded.

In the discussions with students, I deliberately focused on keeping things as relaxed and informal as possible, so there were no set questions to work through, just a series of topics I was keen to explore, including sex, alcohol, drugs, peer relationships, parental control and future pathways. The students were seen in classroom groups and the discussions lasted for the duration of the set period I'd been allocated, usually between 45 and 60 minutes. I talked with approximately 180 classes of boys ranging from (in Australian equivalents) Year 7 (the first year of high school) to Year 12 (the last year). (New Zealand high school covers five rather than six years, running from Years 9 to 13: Year 13 there is equivalent to Years 11 and 12 in Australia.) The majority of the discussions were held with more senior students.

It quickly became apparent that if I was to get the best from the boys, I could neither write down nor record the discussion. In the first few classroom meetings, whenever I paused to scribble down a particularly humorous quote (of which there were many), I immediately noticed that I'd just lost my audience and it always took a few minutes to get them back. In time I learned to hold the quote in my head until the bell rang and the students plunged noisily from the room. Fortunately the quotes were so memorable that it wasn't hard to keep them within mental range until pen and paper were available. This was in fact my first lesson within the project: the boys responded best to roving eye contact, which reassured them that what they were saying mattered and was OK, acceptable, even important.

I enjoyed my time in the classrooms immensely. The students handed me some amazing information, though they often had no real awareness of the importance and value of what they were communicating. On occasion they were so candid in expressing their views that I'd be almost paralytic with laughter; they had no idea why this middle-aged woman was standing in front of them laughing her head off, but I can definitely recall struggling to get my breath, they were so funny.

The junior students were insightful and their humour and approach to life shed a great deal of light on the maturation process of boys. The Year 9 students presented major challenges in terms of maintaining any semblance of control of the discussion and the classroom, but also provided extraordinary insights. But it was the discussions with senior students that had the real potential to produce answers to the questions that had prompted the project. It was in these classes I struck gold and understood just what potential lies within young men making their way towards adulthood.

I didn't seek the students' permission to involve them in the project, principally because most of them displayed a very keen interest from the moment the idea was raised with them. Before I arrived, their teacher had explained why the class would be following a different format that day and given that the alternative was taking part in, for example, a physics or an English lesson, it came as no surprise that I was always welcomed with enthusiasm. Any student who didn't want to take part in the discussion could simply remain silent and some did, although, in the end, not many. A number of students didn't talk directly to me, but almost all appeared to talk to their fellow classmates about the ideas being discussed.

After an introduction to the reasons behind the project, I usually initiated discussion by asking the students why they were at a boys' school and what they saw as the main differences between themselves and girls of their age — other than the obvious physical ones, I was always quick to add.

On a few occasions some of the students tried to check just how many of the basic biological differences between men and women I was aware of. When that happened, I was always quick to assure them that I'd done my own research in that regard over a number of years and didn't need their help to clarify matters. Their reaction at that point was usually to put their hands over their faces and groan: the idea of a woman of my age having been involved in such research was obviously a little too hard to digest.

Discussion tended to flow within a very short time of my arrival, going off on a number of tangents, but always coming back to their relationships with their parents, with girls and with their peers, the alcohol and drug scene, their ideas about what makes a good man and who in their lives they considered to be good men.

Rather than attempting to lead the conversation in any one particular direction, I let it take its own course, usually with delightful results. The discussion would often amble around the room without much apparent focus until a wonderful one-liner would emerge, usually from a student who hadn't appeared to be particularly connected to the discussion. As the session drew to a close, I would attempt to pick up the threads of the discussion and plug the gaps in the information they'd given me by asking some slightly more focused questions. This wasn't always successful though. They were having such a good time exploring the issues I'd raised that they often resisted any attempt to tie the conversation down.

In the course of their introduction to the project, I spoke to the students about the time I'd spent working inside prisons and raised with them the idea that many young New Zealand men, young men just like them, seem to enter prison as part of proving their manhood. The mention of the word 'prison' guaranteed the students' immediate attention and they were always very keen to hear any prison stories I was willing to tell.

I didn't hold back in my descriptions of prison life and often pondered what the conversations over the dinner table at home that night might have been like and whether parents wondered just what their sons had been learning at school that day. Of course this fleeting concern applied only to the more junior students, boys who were still in the habit of telling their parents about their day. I had no doubt that little or nothing would be discussed by the older students, given that adolescent boys and talk at the dinner table very rarely go together, especially when the boy is in the Year 8 and 9 monosyllabic grunting stage. I was pretty safe really.

One of the trade-offs (aka bribes) I used in the classrooms was to suggest that if the students answered my questions, and talked about what I wanted to talk about, then just before the end of the time available, I was willing to stop the discussion and allow them to ask any question they had about prison and what happens there. This technique proved very useful in terms of focusing the boys' attention on the conversation I wanted to have.

In about 90, if not 99, per cent of the classroom discussions, the first question a student asked about prison was, 'Is it dangerous to bend over for the soap in the shower?' Although I'd said that the questions about prison would come at the end of the session, on some occasions, especially when working with Year 9 boys, I had to answer one question up front to prove that I intended to keep my promise and that this wasn't just another piece of conning by an adult. And sometimes in the more prestigious schools, where there's a strong emphasis on what does and does not constitute polite behaviour, I would have to both ask and answer the question in order to put the boys out of their misery and move the discussion on. 'Is this the question you would like to know the answer to . . . ?' 'Oh, yes please' would be the response, followed by a sigh of relief that the dilemma was over.

> In about 90, if not 99, per cent of the classroom discussions, the first question a student asked about prison was, 'Is it dangerous to bend over for the soap in the shower?'

I always answered a very emphatic 'Yes' to the soap question — in my view, any deterrent to prison is a good deterrent — but then went on to explain the facts about life in prison a little more realistically than most American prison movies do. It isn't as common an occurrence as the movies suggest, staff don't watch, it doesn't only happen in the shower — these were the sorts of issues we explored once the topic was up for discussion. Separate to the matter of possible sexual assault, I wanted the students to understand that ultimately it would be their choice whether they ever saw the inside of a prison cell; my work experience suggested they shouldn't want to.

Was there any potential conflict in a woman spending time in boys' schools discussing the concept of a good man and what might constitute legitimate and effective male rites of passage? It is, after all, men's business and should remain so. This aspect of the project was canvassed fully with the principals in the initial discussions as the project brief took shape and I was fully aware of it as I began the school visits. At each opening staff briefing I explained that I was there not to talk but to *listen* to both the students and the staff as they described the world of boys' schools. I then had to place what I was told and what I was able to observe within the context of the alternative rite of passage, the journey to prison, and to hold up a mirror so that the teachers and parents of adolescent boys could see, as I had, the potential of boys' schools to positively affect the choices made by boys in their quest for manhood.

My job was only to collect the stories and hold up the mirror. It was not then, and nor is it now, to translate for men what they're seeing in the mirror or to tell them what to do next. I can describe what the world of men looks like from my perspective, but it must always be remembered and acknowledged that my perspective is that of a woman looking into the world of men.

Because I've been a single parent who brought up a son, I have no qualms telling women what they might like to consider doing differently in raising their boys as a result of my experience with the Good Man Project. That, in fact, is the primary reason for this book. I'm also very clear, however, that having held up the mirror for both men and women to see what I was lucky enough to see, my job is almost over. The bulk of what now needs to be done is men's work and men must be allowed to get on with it. And get on with it they will, if we women have the courage and the willingness to stand back and allow them to do so.

The Good Man Project was a gift, a very special gift, that allowed me entry to, and changed forever my perception of, the world of boys' schools and the world of men. Before I move on to describe what I learned, I want to pause and say a heartfelt thank you to all those involved. It was a memorable time and I owe an enormous debt of gratitude to those who travelled the road with me.

Chapter 2
The Wonderful World of Boys' Schools

Before the Good Man Project, I thought, as many others appear to, that most boys' schools were part of the 'old school tie' network, focused primarily on ensuring that their students gained the necessary business and social connections to smooth their path through life. I also considered it likely that the more prestigious the school, the more any incoming student would have to fit the school rather than vice versa.

I was willing to concede that there was some potential value in single-sex education for boys: I had, after all, sent my own son to a Catholic boys' secondary school for what I thought at the time were a number of well-considered reasons. Interestingly, those reasons are now more than a little unclear. But although I saw enough advantages in single-sex education to trust my son to it, I remained unconvinced that boys' schools were reaching their full potential in exploring the reality of manhood in today's world. I'd been impressed with what I saw when I spent some time at Nelson College in 2001 as part of the project about the management of behaviourally challenging students in the classroom, but that visit didn't substantially alter my generally negative view.

When I attended the meeting of Heads of Boys' Schools with Salvi Gargiulo in September 2001, I was certain that these men, the guardians of the bastions of traditional boys' schools, were unlikely to have anything to say that I would find at all interesting or challenging. How wrong I was. At that point I began a journey that has taught me much, unravelled my prejudices and left me with a strong sense of magic about the schools where boys can just be boys and where the business of boys is the sole focus.

This isn't to say there's no room for improvement in the way boys' schools prepare their students for the world — that was why the project was born — but they do a great number of things exceptionally well.

By their very existence boys' schools encourage the building of a sense of pride in being male. In a world where there's a great deal of discussion about the absence of positive male role models and where much of the media focus is on the more negative aspects of young men, the ability of boys' schools to provide an alternative view cannot be underestimated.

For many boys who choose to attend a boys' school — or, as many of them would have it, have that choice forced upon them — the initial school assembly will be the first time they've encountered their own gender in such numbers and in a totally male-focused environment. When I talked to Year 7 students I could discern their pride in entering a man's world, a world that would offer them a sense of belonging and validation. The message in these schools was clear: to be male is to be OK.

For many students, too, entering such a school means they'll be taught by a man for the first time. Male teachers appear to be a rare commodity in primary schools and it was encouraging to see the numbers and diversity of male teachers in the staffrooms of these secondary schools.

Entry to an all-boys' high school appears to be very much a case of 'welcome to the world of men'. At the beginning of the project I struggled a great deal with the sense of history and tradition visible in the schools, but in time I came to understand its significance in the eyes of the boys themselves. For reasons related to my personal experience, I don't tend to attach a great deal of importance to such things, but there could be no denying how much it was valued by most of the students I met.

At one school I was urged by an obviously proud teacher to visit the library and I wondered at his enthusiastic insistence that I do so. It was in fact a museum containing mementoes from the lives of many of the school's old boys. On one wall hung photos of those who had become judges or taken other high-profile positions in the community; on another were sporting trophies obtained at world events, including the replica of a gold medal won at the Olympic Games by an old boy. It was as I stood in this room and took in the sense of tradition surrounding me that I began to understand more about the essence of maleness. It's about connection, about linkages to the past that show the pathways to the future and it's about excellence, striving to be successful in order to honour those who have gone before. It's about loyalty and hard work and belonging.

As a woman who has spent much of her life wondering what might be around the next corner, I've often rebelled against a system that emphasises clear and strong links to a past I struggle to understand, but I was unable to ignore the sense of pride and anticipation discernible among junior students as we discussed what it meant to be a member of their school. Although many of them had come to the school at the behest of their parents, if offered the chance to be elsewhere all but a very few wanted to stay and continue the journey they'd begun.

It became apparent very early on in the project that one of the inherent strengths of boys' schools is their ability to revel in and celebrate the business of boys. In a world that's becoming increasingly hamstrung by political correctness and the reluctance of many in positions of power and influence to call a spade a spade, the freedom available within boys' schools to focus completely on boys' issues is extremely valuable. There's a kind of purity involved when boys can concentrate solely on what matters and is relevant to them at this stage of their lives.

It's important to reiterate at this point that the project was never about comparing the merits of single-sex versus co-educational schools. On the contrary, it was intended to stimulate discussion about the needs of boys in today's world and to see how we can improve the delivery of appropriate life skills to all boys making their way through the education system. Boys' schools and those working in them are extremely well positioned to lead this discussion and all those involved in the lives of adolescent boys, including those working in co-educational secondary schools, can and should make a contribution. I have no doubt whatsoever that the results of any such discussion will be equally applicable to boys attending co-educational and single-sex secondary schools.

Being able to revel in the business of boys isn't only about the absence of girls. The boys' schools I visited showed themselves well able to identify and address the issues of concern to boys, to pursue their specific interests and to provide a setting within which it was safe to explore emotions in a male context. Put simply, there was overt support for being male.

On a number of occasions I observed a course of action being undertaken, usually in relation to the disciplining of a student, and thought to myself, 'I would have done that differently.' If I'm honest, what I really meant was 'I would have done that better.' It took me a while to realise that what I was seeing was men attending to men's business and that I was looking through the eyes of a woman. There's nothing wrong with that, but once I paused long enough to recognise the judgements I was making, I began to develop a keen sense of delight about what happens when men are given this opportunity. The main thing to realise is that it just doesn't look as it would if women were involved — and nor does it need to.

There's no doubt in my mind that men do things differently — this was apparent over and over again throughout the project — but differently doesn't automatically mean either better or worse. This is the trick: to learn to suspend the need for judgement that usually follows any such acknowledgement of difference. As a result of the time spent in boys' schools, I've learnt that silence on a woman's part can often allow the communication channel between an adult man and an adolescent boy to operate more effectively than it does when a woman interrupts the transmission, as we are often wont to do.

In time I came to understand the value in schools where the boys didn't have to concern themselves with their appearance beyond the basics of wearing the correct clothing, tucking their shirts in and pulling their socks up.

The absence of jewellery, hair gel and piercings was one of the first things I noticed.

'No chicks to impress, no need for hair gel.'

Students at all levels talked about the freedom of not having to worry about appearance — because there were no girls — and seemed to consider it a major benefit of being at a boys' school. Demonstrating their innate pragmatism, as they often did, the boys regularly commented that one of the main benefits of not having to worry about, for example, applying hair gel each morning was being able to spend an additional ten minutes in bed. 'No chicks to impress, no need for hair gel.' They agreed that they paid considerable attention to their appearance outside school hours and didn't see themselves as any different in that regard from their peers attending co-educational schools, but they left me with the impression that the absence of pressure about their appearance at school made life a whole lot simpler and allowed them to stay longer in the moment of being boys.

Given this, I found it interesting to watch the debate that ensued when the principal of one state boys' high school I'd recently visited came to public notice for enforcing the school rule of no hair gel. A number of people expressed their opinion via the media and many were critical of the school's stand, some going so far as to make an assumption about what sort of man the principal was. One newspaper description had him cast as a pipe-smoking, tweed-jacketed chap of advanced years clinging to tradition, unable and/or unwilling to enter the modern world. Nothing could be further from the truth. He's in his thirties and in my view, and in the view of many, he's a passionate and dedicated leader who possesses a great deal of insight about what boys' schools should be delivering to their students. His is one of the voices I implicitly trust when it comes to the reality of adolescent boys.

It seemed to me that most students didn't care about the restriction on the use of hair products and usually objected only in their often-quoted context of 'Yeah, I know it's a rule, but I'm going to have a go at breaking it anyway', before turning back and getting on with the things they considered really mattered.

Many of the students I spoke to, including those at that school, talked openly and without ridicule from their classmates of the freedom the school stand on hair and jewellery gave them, and on one occasion when I asked a group of Year 11 and 12 students how long it had taken them to get used to following the rules in this regard, they replied 'about a week'. Some students I spoke to, particularly those in Years 9 and 10 of high school, did struggle with their inability to register their individuality through their appearance and some of my classroom discussions with them did focus on what might be done to allow them a little more leeway, but even these boys also seemed to value the clarity and simplicity of those rules.

> 'Yeah, I know it's a rule, but I'm going to have a go at breaking it anyway.'

It also occurred to me as I monitored the media debate on this issue how many women were condemning the school for its stand, mothers standing up for what they perceived to be the rights of their sons, and how silent the men were. Where were the male voices? And were the mothers taking the issue on face value as presented by their sons, as I'd done many times with my son when arguing with the school, rather than looking beyond the matter at hand to the wider issues of adolescent boys and what they actually need rather than what they want?

The physicality of boys proved to be one of the absolute delights of the project. Standing in a school assembly of 1400 students very quickly grounded me in the reality that is testosterone-driven young men. The noise, the smell, the energy levels and the sheer size of some of the students meant there was never any doubt that I was in a male environment, albeit with some women present.

I'm not an educationalist and many will no doubt have a different view, but it seems to me that anyone who maintains there's little or no difference between boys and girls in terms of their educational requirements need only stand in an all-boy assembly to have their attitude challenged. The differences are palpable and no amount of politically correct analysis will alter them.

On numerous occasions I watched large numbers of boys stream into a school hall and felt a sense of joy at the positive nature of what I was seeing. In previous years I'd watched male inmates gather in prison wings, in work parties and/or on prison parade grounds and had wondered about and grieved for the extraordinary loss of potential I was witnessing. To see the boys' delight in being who and where they were, to feel their exuberance about life itself, was a glimpse of magic.

The boys' entry to the school halls also made me laugh. They appeared to have no real sense of their bodies and no awareness of the world around them. With shirts hanging out, socks down around their ankles, sandals or shoes flapping loosely, they lumbered around or over chairs, jostled one another and, in what appeared to be a totally unfocused way, eventually found their way to their allocated seat. They often had food in their hands (and mouths) — I've found there's never much distance between adolescent boys and food — and while they seemed able to eat and walk at the same time, they appeared incapable of doing much else or of doing anything at all at speed.

As always with boys, time was the main ingredient, time to allow them to reach their ultimate destination with just the occasional bit of prodding along the way. Hurrying them simply didn't work and an attempt to do so often made things worse since it seemed to lift energy levels and encourage their playful assaults on other students. Rather than explaining to the boys where they needed to be, something the female teachers present repeatedly tried to do, the male teachers seemed to instinctively know that the best plan was to position themselves like sheep dogs, guarding the boundaries and nudging the boys slowly and gently forward towards their allocated seats.

The physicality of the boys regularly overwhelmed me, as I'm sure it does their teachers from time to time. It was most evident in Year 9 and when talking to teachers involved with students at this level, I often commented that the most effective technique for controlling them, while trying to get at least a few scraps of information into their heads, might be to allow them to stand up every ten minutes and put someone in a headlock before sitting down again.

I have to admit that as a result of spending several school periods trying to engage in a meaningful way with boys at this level, I also began to wonder about the potential benefits of reintroducing the cane just for that year. The value of grounding them with a physical experience took on definite appeal in the face of their exuberance and inability to concentrate for more than 30 seconds — and that only if the subject fell within their somewhat limited classification of interesting.

In a class of such students, it was possible to actually see the levels of testosterone begin to rise and, as they did, to realise how impossible it was becoming for the boys to sit still. It was like watching a wave build from the back of the room and I sometimes felt the need to pause, duck and let the water roll over my head before carrying on with the conversation. Boys at this level, and to a lesser degree in the years either side, appeared completely unable to resist the temptation to flick anyone who came within arm's reach with a ruler or to move past a fellow student without hitting him. Asking them why they behaved this way often led to a look that suggested I'd questioned their need to inhale oxygen.

If they're ever going to learn anything, boys do need to learn to behave less boisterously on occasion, to be able to control themselves for at least part of their time in the classroom. Teachers and I often discussed possible ways of achieving this. Although this remains an ongoing challenge for those involved in the teaching of boys, I came to appreciate that the all-male environment was somehow able to provide both the space and the opportunity for boys to get the rough and tumble out of their system and move on rather than simply suppressing it in order to meet the expectations of the adults around them. While on occasion I struggled with the physicality of the boys, I frequently observed them being positively and actively managed through their exuberance and into moments of quiet reflection by very skilled teaching staff.

In my previous life, I'd noted that sport appeared to play a major part in the lives of adolescent boys, but in the initial stages of the project I wasn't willing to consider it as anything other than a side issue. My time in boys' schools significantly challenged my views in this regard and led me to realise that sport is something boys' schools both do exceedingly well and use very effectively in their management of the students. In my discussions with the boys themselves, I came to understand that, for the vast majority of boys, sport is an integral part of the journey to manhood both because of its competitive nature and because it can give them a sense of being a part of something bigger than themselves. Most boys' schools can provide a wide range of sporting opportunities that allow their students to experience success and develop a sense of pride. Sport also means they can continue to build a positive relationship with their body and use their high energy levels in a positive way.

I particularly liked the way one teacher explained it: 'Young men have to have a regular adrenaline fix. If they don't get it in the right way, they'll get it in the wrong way. Boys' schools have the capacity to and do provide heaps of the right type of adrenaline.'

In addition to the formal sporting opportunities available, I noted the freedom students at boys' schools appeared to have to play and as the project progressed I became increasingly intrigued by what I saw occurring during morning interval and lunchtime breaks on the school campuses.

When the bell signalling a break in the teaching regime rang, the students would swarm out onto the school grounds and all manner of games would begin. Some were the more traditional games of soccer, rugby and basketball, but there were also numerous games that appeared to be made up on the spot, depending on the number of students wanting to play, the range of equipment at hand and the space available.

The atmosphere seemed to encourage the students to play regardless of their year level and through the mechanism of play the schools appeared able to accommodate and support the frequent dashes maturing students make between the gateway of childhood they're moving away from and the gateway to manhood they're inexorably approaching.

I've often encountered the negative view that boys' schools produce men who are unable to relate to women and who, because of their arrogance about being male — encouraged by the school — carry negative perceptions about the place of women in today's society. At the very least, it has been suggested, the boys leaving such schools are emotionally bereft and incapable of establishing and maintaining effective personal relationships with women. As one former principal of a co-educational school put it, he'd grown sick of having to be a 'finishing school' for those boys who had been educated for four years at a single-sex school, but who then came to him for their final year to learn how to socialise with girls.

Although I didn't necessarily hold quite that view before I embarked on the project, I did have some reservations about the ability of boys' schools to produce emotionally confident young men. My son certainly hadn't appeared to suffer any form of emotional or social retardation as a result of his time at a boys' school — quite the contrary in fact — but I told myself that he'd developed his emotional confidence in spite of the school rather than because of it. He was who he was because of the excellent work done by his mother!

It was common for the fathers of some students, men who had themselves been educated at boys' schools, to reflect that they'd been unable to understand or communicate effectively with members of the opposite sex when they left school. Some of them went on to concede that the workings of the female brain remained a mystery to this day and I have no doubt they're not alone in holding that view.

Their adolescent sons didn't, however, appear to share their experience of not being able to communicate effectively with adolescent girls. Partly due no doubt to the greater degree of social freedom available to girls today, the boys appeared to understand their female counterparts much better than their fathers had. Almost all the boys I spoke to had close female friends within their immediate peer group — often referred to as 'chick-mates' — and many boys spoke of the value of the conversations they had with these girl friends about the 'real' stuff, the stuff they could not or would not talk about with their male peers.

It's true that the boys expressed considerable nervousness about approaching a girl they considered to be 'hot' and were clear in their assertions that the thinking processes of girls were sometimes too hard to follow, but I saw and heard nothing that led me to believe these boys were any different in this regard from their peers attending co-educational schools.

The conversations I had about the likely impact of having girls in the classroom, or in some cases, the reality of actually having girls in the classroom, as happened at the senior levels of some schools, provoked a great deal of discussion and thought about the socialising process that occurs between adolescent boys and girls.

Many teachers who had also taught in co-educational schools commented on the way adolescent boys appeared to modify their behaviour in the face of scorn or criticism from female classmates. During his first two high school years in particular, when a boy often races between acting like a child and acting like a young adult, the censure or potential censure of a female student would cause him to curb his behaviour. 'Sit down and stop being a dick' is apparently a common cry from the girls in co-educational classrooms at the more junior levels.

The boys themselves often spoke of not wanting to appear a fool in front of girls and of how the concern that they might do just that made them quieter in the presence of girls. 'Better to be thought a fool than to open your mouth and remove all doubt' was a concept they seemed to have fully grasped, even if they couldn't express it as clearly as that. When we talked about alcohol they often expressed their anxiety about appearing a fool in front of a girl and explained that one reason for drinking to excess was to gain the necessary confidence to talk in an uninhibited fashion to the 'really hot chicks'.

Almost all Year 7, 8 and 9 students I spoke to felt the presence of girls would make them much less willing to participate in classroom discussions and that in such circumstances their behaviour would 'tone down' and become less boisterous.

Given this, I found myself wondering whether what actually occurs in the classrooms of co-educational schools is an education of boys about girls' expectations of their behaviour, rather than a gender-neutral socialising process. It seemed to me entirely possible that the value judgement of the girls about what does and doesn't constitute OK behaviour might be the major benchmark in the socialising that was taking place. When we talk about the boys at co-educational schools being more socially adept, more 'mature', are we in fact saying that they've learnt earlier than boys educated in single-sex schools just what expectations women have of them? Have they simply learnt to do what we women want of them and is this what we're classifying as maturity? It's an interesting question.

Whether or not that's the case, the more senior students in the boys' schools demonstrated a clear ability to get on with their work and to behave in socially appropriate ways and there was no hint of a lack of socialisation because they hadn't spent time in classrooms with girls. The boisterous behaviour, the inability to concentrate, the ebb and flow of testosterone clearly visible among Year 9 students, regardless of their academic ability and/or socio-economic background, had disappeared. In its place were groups of delightful and seemingly mature young men exhibiting well-developed social skills and leading what appeared to be very active social lives. There was no hint of the need for a year at 'finishing school'.

Many of the discussions held in the course of the Good Man Project focused on what boys need most as they make their way across the bridge of adolescence. On the basis of what I have observed, whatever else we might include in there, the essential element is time.

They need time to think, time to process new-found emotions and time to make decisions about their future.

They need time to just be, to move freely between boyhood and manhood, returning several times, in the initial flush of adolescence, to a state of boyhood where they'll spend time playing while reflecting at a deeper (and often completely invisible) level on the fact that they're in the process of leaving that boyhood behind.

This, it seems to me, is what boys' schools do best of all. They give their students the time they need, time to come fully into the adolescent experience at their own pace, time to adjust to the fact that life is moving on and taking them with it. And while this process is under way, the schools continue to put positive images of manhood before the boys which tell them and build a sense of anticipation about the world of men.

Having outlined what boys' schools do extremely well, I need to emphasise that there's definitely room for improvement and development in a number of areas. I'm not describing a perfect world. The commitment of the principals involved in the Good Man Project and their willingness to let me loose in their schools — a sign of courage, some would say — showed their willingness to learn new things and to listen to suggestions.

The aim isn't perfection; the focus is challenge and investigation and debate, and within the corridors of the boys' schools I visited, I found all these things. I found laughter and sorrow, movement and noise, reflection and discussion. Above all else I found places where my views about the world of men and what adolescent boys need to make it safely across the bridge of adolescence were challenged and where my faith in the inherent goodness and strength of men was restored.

The journey I was fortunate enough to be able to take into the world of boys' schools has left me with a strong sense of optimism about the future of young men, *if* we can make the most of the opportunities these schools present to learn more about what works for boys.

+ By their very existence boys' schools encourage the building of a sense of pride in being male.

+ Maleness is about connection, about linkages to the past that show the pathways to the future, and it's about excellence, striving to be successful in order to honour those who have gone before. It's about loyalty and hard work and belonging.

+ Boys' schools and those working in them are extremely well positioned to lead this discussion and all those involved in the lives of adolescent boys, including those working in co-educational secondary schools, can and should make a contribution.

+ Boys can eat and walk at the same time, but they appear incapable of doing much else or of doing anything at all at speed.

+ For the vast majority of boys, sport is an integral part of the journey to manhood both because of its competitive nature and because it can give them a sense of being a part of something bigger than themselves.

+ Boys appear to understand their female counterparts much better than their fathers did.

✦ When we talk about the boys at co-educational schools being more socially adept, more 'mature', are we in fact saying that they've learnt earlier than boys educated in single-sex schools just what expectations women have of them?

✦ Adolescent boys need time to think, time to process new-found emotions and time to make decisions about their future.

Chapter 3
About a Boy: Inside Their Heads

Having talked about the world of boys' schools, perhaps the next step is to talk about the world of boys and to begin to share what I've learnt about how their minds work — because work they certainly do, even if, from the outside, nothing much seems to be happening.

It's important to note that I'm offering my interpretation of what I saw while interacting with some 180 classes of boys over an 18-month period. The boys themselves may disagree with my interpretation, as may the men who read this book, and I'll be entirely comfortable should they do so. This is a woman's take on the world of adolescent boys, a take that is coloured by my experiences and natural bias. I'm not trying to in any way prove that I know how it is: rather, my aim is to initiate further discussion about how men and women can work together to raise good men and what we might do to ensure we have as much fun as possible with our sons and grandsons, and with each other, along the way.

As a result of my involvement in the Good Man Project I am very clear about one thing: if I'd known at the time I was raising my son what I know now about adolescent boys and the way they view the world, I'd have done a number of things differently. And even if that had meant adjustments to my way of being and acting that only I knew about, I'm sure it would have made my son's passage through adolescence a little easier on us both. He's grown into a fine man, a good man, but as his mother I suffered moments of extreme angst while he negotiated his adolescent years and I lay awake for more nights than I care to remember wondering whether he would survive long enough to become a man. I'd like to think there wouldn't have been quite so many sleepless nights if I'd understood more clearly just how he viewed the world and what was driving his behaviour.

> 'Girls are always wanting you to commit. Boys like to live in the moment.'

In the discussions I had with students a number of themes emerged that allowed me to get a glimpse into the way boys think and how they process information. These themes can be grouped around three main concepts — their pragmatism, their intuition and their desire to live in the moment. Later chapters will address the impact of their inherent pragmatism and their well-developed intuition on the way they live their lives, but let's take our first step into the world of adolescent boys by considering their love of living in the moment and their inability and/or unwillingness to plan in order to better manage their lives. This facet of the adolescent male psyche led to some very humorous conversations. (In fact most of the discussions held during the project were very funny.)

Whenever I asked the boys about planning, their immediate response was to assert that they don't plan. 'We don't plan because plans never work out anyway.' 'Life's a roller-coaster, so there's no point in planning.'

'Do you ever plan?'

'Nah, not really.'

'Oh yeah, Miss, we plan the weekends.'

'When do you start planning the weekend?'

'Oh about Wednesday.'

'So you know how to plan?'

'Yeah.'

'But you just don't do it?'

'Nah.'

'Girls plan a lot, don't they?'

'Yeah, but they change their minds, don't they?'

'Yes, I guess they do.'

'See, waste of time making the decision in the first place!'

One question I always asked as we moved towards a discussion about how they managed their academic workloads: if they were given an assignment that was due to be handed in on, say, Tuesday morning, when would they do it? Regardless of academic ability and/or socio-economic status, the answer at this point was invariably 'Monday night', with the occasional 'Tuesday morning' thrown in. When I went on to ask if there was anything the adults in their lives could do to persuade them to do it any earlier, they replied without hesitation, 'Yeah, money.'

When I made it clear that payment for assignments was not an option anyone was going to take seriously, we

'Do you think you'll ever have a life plan?

'No'.

'So how will your life sort itself out?'

'Oh that's easy. I'll be about 25 and some gorgeous-looking chick will walk past. She'll have a great plan, so I'll just hook onto her.'

went on to discuss whether they ever considered doing the assignment any earlier than the night before it was due. At this point they were usually at pains to point out that yes, they definitely thought about doing it earlier, sometimes even going so far as to 'pick it up'. When I then asked what stopped them from actually doing some work on it in that moment, the answer was always quite clear: 'There's always something better to do.' The something better included a game to play, a video to watch and/or a mate to hang out with — none of these alternatives particularly pressing, but all more appealing than the waiting assignment. As I eventually came to understand it, the moment to do the assignment had simply not yet arrived.

It was a source of great amusement to me when, on some occasions, I pushed a little harder with the students and suggested that if they only did the assignment the night before anyway, regardless of when it was handed out, perhaps the best idea would be to ask their teachers to adopt the practice of giving out assignments overnight, working to the idea that they would have only the one night to get it done. It seemed a very logical step to me and one that would mean a significant reduction in levels of stress for those parents who spend their lives trying to compel their sons to start work on the assignment due next week.

Whenever I suggested this idea, however, looks of absolute consternation would cross the faces of the boys. 'No, you can't do that.'

'Why not?'

'Because we need time to think about it!'

The boys seemed to survive this stage in their lives by combining their ever-present pragmatism with a touch of fatalism — 'no point in making the decision twice', 'who cares, it will happen anyway' — which allowed them to hold off doing the assignment in the hope that it might yet prove unnecessary. Maybe there would be a flood, an earthquake and/or a major fire overnight so the assignment would never need to be finished and any effort expended up until then would have been a complete waste of time.

This unwillingness to plan isn't all bad news, however. A story told to me by one teacher challenges the view that adolescent males will reach their potential in the classroom only through planning and organised work. This teacher described the time when he'd explained to a group of senior students that they had only five days left in which to complete their art portfolios and that if they didn't manage to do so within that timeframe, they would lose the opportunity to take art the following year. For many of the boys this would have been a major blow as the career paths they were considering required them to continue with their study of art and, perhaps more importantly, it was a subject they both enjoyed and were good at.

> 'Thinking is boring. Who cares? It will happen anyway.'

These were boys who were quite academically capable, but who had shown themselves to be fairly normal adolescent males by working at about 5 per cent of their potential throughout the year. The teacher had previously taught adolescent girls who, in his view, tended to work at about 90 per cent of their potential throughout the school year.

Once the teacher had delivered the news of the impending deadline, the boys seemed to accept the challenge and immediately got to work. They literally lived and breathed their art portfolios for the following five days, spending every hour at the school, taking only occasional breaks to eat and sleep while getting on with the work. In the teacher's words they went from their previous 5 per cent effort to about 250 per cent. Everything else in their lives fell away and nothing else mattered until their portfolios were complete. Although it is possible to imagine the chaos that might have been building in other areas of their lives during this period, the fact remains that they met the deadline and the work they turned out was of a very high standard. The moment had arrived, they responded and the results were excellent.

The boys also seemed to have been changed for the better and to have become more confident as a result of the experience. They'd been tempered by the challenge and had learnt a bit more about who they were and what they were capable of. So, here's a thought worthy of consideration at this point: is it possible that this learning might not have occurred and the high standard of work not been reached had the boys chosen instead to work steadily throughout the year?

Is it possible that the inertia frequently displayed by adolescent boys occurs because the challenges being put in front of them aren't of sufficient depth to merit a real response? That only when the challenge is significant in their eyes, rather than in ours, do they respond to it? Have we made education a series of relatively small steps because we think that's what works, when what boys actually want and need are fewer, much bigger steps? There are many far more qualified than me to answer that question, and no doubt many would disagree with the idea, but several times throughout the project it seemed to me that it is challenge that boys are looking for and need if they're to be fully involved.

As a result of the education I received during the Good

Man Project I've decided that the ability to cut to the chase, to focus on the actual issue rather than on all the associated matters we women might be aware of and seek to consider and manage, is an inherent male trait. We women seem to move in a circle, expanding its edges as we move and drawing in more and more 'stuff'. Men move in a straight line, often ignoring everything that's off to the sides as they focus on what needs to be done. Isn't this in fact what the boys working on their art portfolios did, pushing aside what needed to be pushed aside so they had the time and space to do what needed to be done? They were motivated because the moment had arrived, the deadline was in sight.

The fatalism evident in boys seems to be an adolescent trait, a sign that they don't yet feel any real control over their lives. The world still seems a bit too big and their place in it isn't clear, so they continue to evaluate which adult wants them to do what by when and act accordingly, always mindful of the consequences of non-compliance and playing their own game of chance. It's a way of making their world manageable (and more interesting) during a period when they still believe it doesn't really matter what they do, despite what those around them are saying.

Wherever I looked in my discussions with adolescent boys, linked to their ability to focus only on what needed to be done and their sense that there was no point in planning anything other than the next weekend's social activities was their clearly discernible desire to live completely in the moment. Again and again they demonstrated, by both their actions and their words, that being fully in the moment is what matters; in fact it's often the only thing that matters.

At one school a group of senior students led the discussion

around to the topic of death and grief and from there on to the issue of youth suicide. I suggested that in my experience many young men decided to end their lives because they were trapped in a phase of despair and could see no way out: in such cases it was living in the moment, as so many young men do, that had proven fatal. One student agreed, adding 'but we like living in the moment'. I confirmed that this was part of what made boys gorgeous, but then went on to ask whether he could understand how frightening we adults find the implications of some of the decisions made by the young men we love in their more vulnerable moments.

> 'You just have to keep telling us there'll be more moments.'

He acknowledged that he could understand our fear so I then asked him what he would tell despairing young men if he was one of us, the concerned adults. Without hesitation, and with extraordinary wisdom, he replied, 'You just have to keep telling us there'll be more moments.'

From the discussions I had with the students I concluded that fear of failure is one of the things that keeps them living in the moment longer than those of us who love them might wish. Fear of failure featured regularly in the conversations and was often given as a reason for not trying. Notably, it was raised most often in the context of competition with girls.

In the words of one teacher, 'Boys often won't have a go unless their success or a return is guaranteed. They constantly analyse the risk in terms of being made to look silly and won't put their heads above the parapet if there's the slightest chance of it being shot off.'

If there was any suggestion that they'd come second to a

girl in something they were about to do, the boys admitted they would simply not try rather than risk failure. On a number of occasions, I gained the impression that they felt the world was stacked against them: girls were perceived to be better students because they were tidier in their work and paid more attention to detail, and the external world favoured women over men. This wasn't a perception held by all the students I spoke to, but it was common enough to give some cause for concern about the message we're giving adolescent boys. There's a fine line between the perception that girls learn differently from boys and the perception that they learn better. The boys often appeared to be receiving the latter message.

As discussions continued, I began to connect their fear of failure not only to their desire to live in the moment, but also to their unwillingness to plan. It seems to me now that all three are inextricably linked. Consider this discussion with 20 academically capable senior students just a few months before they were due to leave school:

'How many of you know what you're going to do next year?'

Twenty hands went up.

'How many of you are going on to tertiary study?'

Twenty hands went up.

'How many of you know what course you're going to do?'

Twenty hands went up.

'How many of you know what jobs you want?'

Three hands went up.

Surprised by the sudden change in numbers, I backtracked and asked how it was that they knew what course they were going to do, but didn't know what job they wanted. The answer came back immediately: 'You've got to keep your options open.'

Is it about keeping their options open or is it about avoiding the possibility of failure? As one student said in the ensuing discussion, 'The job you want mightn't be there when you've finished studying, so it's best not to think too far ahead.' If, for example, he wants to be a pilot and he's open about that and then doesn't make it, for whatever reason, he's deemed both by himself and others, possibly more particularly by himself, to have failed and his self-esteem takes a backward step. In the words of one teacher, 'Boys have dreams, but their risk of failure keeps them from going too close until they're mature enough to be able to cope with the possibility of failure. They consider it better not to try than to try and fail.' In the view of this adult man it's only in their thirties that men become willing, and able, to cope with the possibility of failure.

> 'The job you want mightn't be there when you've finished studying, so it's best not to think too far ahead.'

Little boys talk openly about what they want to be when they grow up, but during the project very few boys declared their dreams and those who did, did so very quietly. The majority of adolescent girls I've met seem to talk freely about their dreams for the future or, at the very least, can be easily persuaded to discuss possible future directions. They may, as the boys pointed out, change their minds a number of times, but they generally have some idea of where they're going and how they're going to get there. Do boys really have no idea where they're heading? Are they quite happy to deal with this issue when the moment arrives, or do a significant number keep silent about their hopes and dreams through a fear of failure? Is living in the moment the safest place for an adolescent boy?

As a result of the classroom discussions I came to believe that adolescent boys are considerably less resilient than girls of the same age. There were moments during the project when their vulnerability washed over me and I found myself wondering how we actually manage to get so many of them safely through to manhood. They often left me with the impression they were accidents waiting to happen. Their childlike naivety (which many of them seem to hold on to longer than girls), their dependence on their peers to define their behaviour, their desire to live in the moment and their associated unwillingness to plan all combine at a time when male hormones are raging through their bodies and the blood appears to be flowing down rather than up. It's a potent mix and one that leaves adolescent boys extremely vulnerable, despite their outwardly strong physical appearance.

A regular topic of discussion was the management and processing of emotion. As we talked it became apparent that the only really acceptable emotion adolescent boys feel able to display is anger. Any other potentially negative emotion, such as grief, hurt or sadness, is transmuted into anger and dealt with accordingly, and when I asked the boys how they dealt with anger, the answer was invariably 'hit something . . . or someone'.

As we'll see later when I talk about Year 12 boys, the senior students were able to provide a variety of images in relation to anger and grief. They were very clear that only time reduces such emotions and that nothing can be done to hasten the process. They explained that moving away from whatever emotion they are feeling allows them to detach themselves from it and eventually let it go: in that moment it loses its power. They were adamant that talking doesn't generally help and couldn't be persuaded otherwise. As one student put it, 'We do feel emotions deeply, but we actually don't need to always be talking about it.' They seemed to believe that, given time, the hard knocks of life become manageable and life can move on, but that this process can't be hurried.

In time I came to understand that the idea of not needing to talk about some difficult or stressful situation wasn't part of a male conspiracy to keep information away from women — at least not always. Sometimes it really is true that males, both adolescent boys and adult men, don't want or need to talk. They just want time to let the conflicting emotions settle until they can make some sense of them and get a grip on what they're feeling. Unlike me, they don't work out what they're feeling by talking about it. They work it out and then — sometimes — talk about it.

When the students were asked if and when it was OK to cry, they gave a variety of answers, many of them extremely humorous: 'When your eyes are full of mace' or 'Crying is OK for stuff that matters — like when your son crashes your Ferrari.' Generally, though, the standard answer was 'when someone dies'. Some boys talked of having seen adult men, including their fathers, cry (usually at funerals or immediately after the death of a family member or close friend), but most hadn't and didn't regard it as natural male behaviour.

> 'We do feel emotions deeply, but we actually don't need to always be talking about it.'

When I asked what message they might have been given about crying as children, the majority agreed that the 'boys don't cry' concept had been there, though not always as an overt statement. Sometimes it was the sense of disapproval they picked up when they did cry that persuaded them it was time to stop. Most of them had experienced such sayings as 'Don't be a girl'. When I asked when they first began receiving negative messages about crying, some said as young as six or seven, but the more common answer was around ten years of age.

The boys themselves offered some interesting insights into men crying and whether they'd stopped because they'd been told to and so were denying a natural impulse, or because they no longer felt the need to cry. Before undertaking the project, I tended to believe it was the former, that men have as natural an instinct to cry as women and that they learn not to cry as adult males in order to meet society's expectations. Now I'm not quite so sure.

> 'Crying is OK for stuff that matters — like when your son crashes your Ferrari.'

The boys talked of not crying in movies not because it wasn't sad, but because it wasn't 'real'. (One particularly articulate boy added at this point that comforting girls crying in movies provided a 'good way to move in'. He moved his arm up into a semi-circle as if wrapping it around a girl's shoulders to show me what he meant.) They talked of not crying when they hurt themselves because, as one student clearly put it when speaking of a broken arm, 'The pain was there', pointing to his arm, 'while crying is here', pointing to his heart, and 'they're not connected' — making it clear that for him crying isn't an instinctive reaction. When asked how they did react when they hurt themselves, they inevitably replied 'swearing'.

They also talked of having stopped crying when it was no longer a way of ensuring they got attention and/or their own way. When we discussed their crying as little boys if they fell over and scraped their knees or tumbled out of trees, they identified crying in those circumstances as largely a reaction to the shock of what had happened and/or a means of getting attention: their crying started for the first reason and was carried on for the second. They explained that the effectiveness of this kind of crying eventually wore off so they stopped and found other ways to get attention. And, as one student put it, 'Crying doesn't change anything, it just leaves you breathless.'

> 'Crying doesn't change anything, it just leaves you breathless.'

Loyalty was a characteristic the students often associated with the concept of a good man; it seemed to be an important facet of their world. When I asked what loyalty looked like, I was told this: 'When a big bastard is coming towards you and you know you're going to get a hiding, but your mate stays with you and gets a hiding too.' My response to this idea was to suggest that it sounded a lot like stupidity to me, but I was assured it was in fact loyalty and that every man and adolescent boy would recognise it as such. I found myself wondering at that point whether loyalty was also the boy who puts his foot down on the accelerator and runs an orange traffic light when encouraged to do so by his mates in the back seat and loses his life, and possibly theirs, as a result.

> 'We get over stuff. We keep our friends.'

Loyalty to their mates appeared to be the basis for many of the actions taken by the students and seemed to add considerable weight to the potential influence of their peer group. Whenever they were asked who they took guidance from, who knew the most about the fabric of their lives and who mattered to them the most, the answer was always 'my mates'.

I often wondered how much that might change once they became involved with girls, but was repeatedly

> 'Loyalty is when a big bastard is coming towards you and you know you're going to get a hiding, but your mate stays with you and gets a hiding too.'

assured that it was 'mates before dates' or, in some schools, 'bros before hoes'. Only among some Year 11 and 12 students was there any recognition that a relationship with a girl might take precedence over one with a mate, and even then it was dubious.

As one senior student said, 'You can always get a girl, but you can't always get a good friend.'

According to another older boy, 'Girls don't really feature. There's too much planning involved in keeping them happy and meeting the responsibilities of the relationship.'

Interestingly, despite their stated view that mates came first, the boys also conceded that they didn't discuss the real stuff of life with their friends because they didn't trust that what they said wouldn't get out and be spread around the school. They would talk to their mates about acceptable emotions such as anger, but they would hold in the other softer emotions such as being in love or being scared unless or until they could talk them over with a girl. They said they did this because 'she won't tell anyone', whereas anything they told even their best mate would eventually find its way into the wider school community.

I struggled with this apparent contradiction. They put their mates before girls, they declared that one of the differences between them and girls was that they, the boys, kept their friends and they talked constantly about loyalty, yet they entrusted their deepest secrets about their emotions only to the girls in their lives, assuming that anything they told their mates would eventually become public knowledge. I'm still not sure how these two realities can exist side by side and can only assume that, in the minds of the boys, loyalty isn't about keeping secrets, but rather about having someone standing at your side as you meet the challenges you're constantly seeking as an adolescent boy.

'Chicks think too much during conversations.'

'Girls are always analysing things. Guys — if it's not broke, don't fix it.'

'They talk about stuff we don't want to hear — what moisturiser works, what colour their bedroom's painted.'

'Guys, they tell you what they're thinking. Girls, you've got to read their minds because there's no way in hell they're going to tell you what they're thinking.'

This apparent emphasis on loyalty among the boys led me to think about the impact of peer pressure or what I now prefer to call horizontal learning. Throughout these adolescent years it appeared to be almost entirely through observing their peers, with the assistance of their intuition, that the students were learning what was and wasn't OK. This was particularly true of

Year 9 students, who were right out on their own in terms of their ability to dismiss everyone other than their peer group as wankers, losers or dorks, but even the older students, who appeared more willing and able to accept advice and input from other adults, still filtered that advice and input through the attitude of their peers.

The students watched what happened as 'he' did this or said that and if it got a positive response from the rest of the peer group, they stored it away as a word or action they would use at some later date when there was a need to appear cool. If another student made a fool of himself in some way, they made a mental note never to do what he had done. If a member of their peer group noted that a certain teacher was 'OK' or a 'dickhead', there was usually a general murmur of agreement.

Rather than seeing peer pressure as a negative force, I began to see it as having considerable potential for good if we can learn to use the channels it provides to bring adolescent boys the right sort of information. Perhaps we just need to learn to use the filter of their peers' attitude more effectively than we currently do. It seems to me we, the adults in the lives of adolescent boys, expend a great deal of energy pushing against peer pressure rather than seeking to use it for our own ends: to keep the young men we love safe; to challenge them in positive ways as they make their way across the bridge of adolescence; and to help them grow into the good men they have the potential to be.

The inner workings of the minds of adolescent boys continue to be a source of amazement (and amusement) to me, as I'm sure they are to many of those struggling with a son who has suddenly become a monosyllabic grunter. It may appear nothing much is happening inside his head, but the project taught me the opposite: a great deal is going on. Our peace of mind lies in our ability to trust the process, to know he won't be this way forever and to learn to recognise what we're seeing and why he's behaving the way he is. Getting ourselves to this place will allow us to enjoy him and to laugh with him — and there's a lot of laughter waiting.

+ Recognise their desire to live in the moment, their inability and/or unwillingness to plan their lives.

+ Have we made education a series of relatively small steps because we think that's what works, when what boys actually want and need are fewer, much bigger steps?

+ The fatalism evident in boys seems to be an adolescent trait, a sign that they don't yet feel any real control over their lives.

+ Fear of failure keeps boys living in the moment longer than those of us who love them might wish.

+ There's a fine line between the perception that girls learn differently from boys and the perception that they learn better.

+ Boys are considerably less resilient than girls of the same age.

+ The only really acceptable emotion adolescent boys feel able to display is anger.

✦ Boys often associate loyalty with the concept of a good man; it's an important facet of their world.

✦ They'll talk to their mates about acceptable emotions such as anger, but hold in the other softer emotions until they can talk them over with a girl.

✦ Never underestimate the power of peer pressure, or horizontal learning, for adolescent boys.

Chapter 4
The Bridge of Adolescence: Years 7 to 12

I've already referred a number of times to the bridge of adolescence. Perhaps it's time to explain the idea in more detail.

This concept had often occurred to me during the raising of my daughter and son. As I approached the bridge with my daughter, the elder of my two children, I was aware that we were entering a new stage in her life but had a sense it was all right to walk onto the bridge with her. She was a girl and her journey across the bridge would make her a woman. I'm a woman and whatever our differing views of the world, whatever path in life she was going to choose, we were destined always to have a great deal in common. Being able to stand on the bridge of adolescence together didn't make the journey all sweetness and light. At times she was running ahead of me with enthusiasm; at others she was walking behind me, sulking spectacularly as only adolescent girls can (and usually for no other reason than you'd held your face the wrong way that morning, or perhaps because this was the day when she'd wondered just why God had made you her mother). But for a significant part of the journey we walked side by side and occasionally we even managed to hold hands.

The Bridge of Adolescence

That wasn't the case with my son. As the bridge of adolescence loomed, I felt I shouldn't be going onto it with him. He was on his way to manhood, a concept I barely understood, and I knew I wouldn't and couldn't understand parts of the journey he was about to undertake. I was proud of the special mother-son relationship I felt we enjoyed, but I knew that if he was to become a man, a good man, we would need to separate for a time. But I wrestled with a problem as we drew close to the bridge: if I couldn't go onto it with him, who was going to? His father wasn't a major feature in his life at that time and although there were some good men in my life, the challenge was to find ways of having these and/or other good men more directly involved in my son's life. I'll talk more later of the challenges faced by mothers raising sons without fathers, but suffice to say that as my son was running towards the bridge of adolescence, far too early in my view and at breakneck speed, I felt obliged to walk up onto the bridge even while recognising at some deep intuitive level that I shouldn't be there.

As we'll see, this is the central issue in the lives of adolescent boys: how to get mothers off the bridge and fathers onto it. Mothers do need to step back; there does come a moment when the level of direct involvement in the lives of our sons needs to ease a little in order to assist their passage into manhood. One thing is clear, however: if there isn't a man clearly visible at the edge of the bridge into whose care they can entrust their sons, mothers will walk onto the bridge. They won't abandon their boys. The challenge for fathers is to make themselves clearly visible at the edge of the bridge so they can be seen by both their sons and their wives or partners and so there is plenty of time for all involved to adjust to the impending change.

And this is surprisingly easy if we just pause and listen to what the boys themselves are saying.

The challenge to mothers is to willingly usher their sons onto the bridge knowing that, for a time, he'll be on a journey they can watch only from a distance. It's not about mothers abandoning their sons; it's about them accepting that for a time they will walk beside the bridge of adolescence rather than on it, or if they can't quite manage to stay off the bridge, that they at least commit to walking on one side rather than marching down the centre line directing traffic, as I spent much of my time doing. This, too, is surprisingly easy if we just pause and listen to what the boys themselves are saying, although in my experience the boys end up having to say it a little more emphatically because of their mothers' perception that they know best what their beloved sons need.

For now let's return to the issue of what boys might need (as opposed to want) as they move through the various stages of adolescence.

It's apparent to all who work with them that boys like clear boundaries: they like to know what's being required of them and by whom and what will happen to them if they don't do what's being asked. They like things to be kept simple and they're extremely pragmatic when assessing whether they'll do something. Given this, and the fact that in their early adolescent years they'll be swamped with testosterone, it seems entirely appropriate that in the early stages of their secondary school career, boys don't have a lot of discretion about school rules and the way the school does things.

During my time in the classrooms of the various schools, I began to develop a mental picture of boys' education and what boys need to assist their learning and to keep them safe as they move forward on their journey.

These were the questions I initially posed for myself as I sought some sort of visual image that explained what I was seeing: if we were bringing a group of boys into a room in which they were going to spend the next six years of their life, what would the room need to have in it in order to facilitate their learning? How is the room different because boys rather than girls are being educated in it? What changes would need to occur in the room over the six years to accommodate the growth process the boys will go through? My observations of the boys I met in the classrooms left me with these answers.

As he enters secondary school, a boy requires, in a metaphorical sense, to be brought into a large uncluttered room. Anything that might have been on the floor needs to be lifted up and taken away. There must be a vast amount of space in the room because for the next six years he's going to be on the move, physically, mentally and emotionally. This doesn't mean that he can't be asked to sit at a desk and learn, but his head and quite often his body won't be still unless he's asleep and even then stillness can't be guaranteed. Our ability to educate him and take him towards his unrealised potential will depend on our ability to connect with him while he's on the move. He'll spend almost all his time in the room playing, he'll make physical contact, some of it rough, with almost every boy he meets as he plays and it will be through play rather than by being forced to sit still that he'll learn. His learning will happen while he's mobile.

It's interesting to note, in line with this idea of unceasing movement, that there is a classroom chair designed in New Zealand, and now available in Australia, which takes into account a boy's need to move. The word from some teachers of boys is that this piece of Kiwi ingenuity is working magic in classrooms; a number of female teachers who have to cope with the physicality of boys in their daily lives have been lining up to kiss the designers.

How is the room different because boys rather than girls are being educated in it? In my view, if a girl were going to occupy the room for the next six years, there would need to be a series of pathways laid out in the room. She may not always be able to tell you immediately, but somewhere in the head of an adolescent girl there's always a plan. Today she's going to be a flight attendant, tomorrow an astrophysicist, the next day a vet . . . then it's back to the flight attendant idea. She'll spend much of her adolescence jumping on and off pathways and her motivation to learn will be based on which particular pathway she's on at any one time.

He doesn't want to be on a pathway. Put him on one and he'll immediately jump off. He wants to be able to run and play, to live in the moment and to enjoy the fact that, for now, he's exactly where he needs to be and there's nowhere else he needs to go.

What changes will need to occur in the room over the next six years if we're to accommodate the growth processes the boy will go through? Let's define the changes in line with the year groups he'll make his way through while at secondary school, but as we do so, it's important to bear in mind that, to a significant degree, the changes that will be discussed here are stereotypical. There will always be boys who will move more quickly or more slowly through the various stages and there will be boys who skip some stages completely. What joy it would be to be the mother of a boy who skips the Year 9 stage! Although there will be these differences, I'm confident that the stages of development I'm about to describe are the norm for the majority of adolescent boys, or at least for the boys I was lucky enough to meet and talk to during the project.

Years 7–8

You can still see the boy in a first-year high school student — he's fresh-faced and bushy-tailed, still a boy, still cute. As he arrives at the gates of the secondary school, he's aware that he's starting a new phase of life. His head's up and he's looking towards the senior students. When he enters an all-boys' school it's as if he can see a banner hanging above the door that says, 'Welcome to the world of men'. We need to focus his attention in this moment and hold it there, just for a brief time, holding him steady while we plant the idea in his head that one day he'll be there, one day he'll be a Year 12 student. We need to make the most of this moment because soon his eyes are going to lower and he won't look up again for quite some time. If we can get this idea into his head during his first weeks that the day will come when he too will be a senior student at the school, we'll do a great deal towards making that a reality and do society in general a major favour.

In the course of my time in the boys' schools I became a big fan of the idea of keeping boys at secondary school for six years. It isn't that there won't always be boys who'll leave earlier because of personal circumstances or because of the future pathways they've chosen and I wouldn't want to see a world where boys *have* to stay for the full six years. What I'd like to see is the glass turned up the other way so that the expectation isn't that a boy will do four years at secondary school and might stay for the extra two, but that the majority will do six years and only some boys will leave school early.

The reasons I now hold this view are linked to my prison experience and the realisation that the main thing a boy needs as he makes his way to adulthood is time: time to come to terms with who he is and who he wants to be; time to find his place in the world that awaits him. Regardless of what he might want to do once he leaves school, staying for the full six years gives him the time he needs and holds him steadier than might otherwise be the case while he copes with the turbulence of adolescence. And, if we can hold him steady in that way, we lessen the chances of his turning up at a prison gate because, like so many young men, he made a stupid decision.

As he begins high school, life is extraordinarily simple for a boy. He's focused on only four things: what do I have to do?; when by?; who's in charge?; and what happens if I don't do it? He doesn't want long, detailed explanations about anything; he doesn't want to know why you've imposed the penalty you have or even why you think he should do what you've asked of him.

There is, however, one small adjunct to the 'what happens if I don't'. He needs to know that in administering any penalty for wrong done or expectations not met, the world will be fair. If he does something and the penalty is this, then if Jimmy does it too, the penalty should be the same. He doesn't want an explanation about how Jimmy comes from a difficult family and we really need to go more gently with him: he couldn't give a damn about Jimmy's background and/or whatever reason you might have on hand to justify treating him differently. His version of fairness goes like this: if this is what happens to me when I do or don't do something, that's what should happen to all of us.

The Year 7/8 boy is interested only in having fun and learning, preferably both at the same time. Given that fact, what else do we need to do to more adequately prepare the space we've created for his education? We've lifted everything off the floor in the room to give him the space he needs, but what else does he require? In terms of the things he's most concerned about — what do I have to do and by when — we need to create a clearly visible boundary that runs without a break around the edges of the room.

He needs to know where those edges are, to be able to see them wherever he stands, so the boundary has to be brightly coloured. It also needs to be firm, because he's going to hurl himself into it on a regular basis over the next couple of years and he must be able to bounce off without hurting himself. Think of the vibrant bouncy castle that kids play on in fairgrounds, or maybe a series of large rubber tyres painted in primary colours. Paradoxically, it's only the boundary — the what, for whom, when and what happens — that gives him the freedom to relax into learning. If he can't see the boundary from wherever he's standing in the room, he'll go looking for it and if he doesn't find it, he'll just keep walking and then we, and he, are in trouble. The first part of his journey in Year 7 is walking the boundary, so it's best we get it in place quickly.

As well as being firm and brightly coloured, the boundary needs one more thing: we have to run a small electric current through it. This is just an extra safety precaution. As he walks the boundary for the first time, he'll touch it to check out how it feels, how real it is, and as part of his learning he needs to feel the light tingle in his fingers. It's this that tells him the boundary is real, that the people in his life are watching, that they do care and are genuine in their desire to keep him safe.

In real terms the electric current is the effort that needs to be put into reinforcing again and again that a certain standard of behaviour is expected and that if it isn't delivered, there are very definite consequences. This year is all about sussing out how serious adults are about the rules and expectations of behaviour they're always (in his mind) going on about. As one Year 7 boy put it, 'Yeah, I know it's a rule but I'm going to have a go at breaking it anyway.' A quick zap from the mild electric current running through the boundary focuses his attention and brings him back into the middle of the room where he will begin the learning that awaits him.

Year 9

And so the real journey begins. As he approaches the end of his second year and crosses into Year 9, he starts to demonstrate to all around him, not least his shell-shocked mother, that he now has a very good grip on his world and is keen for the real fun to begin. Suddenly his parents know nothing and anything he's told by an adult is a plot to ruin his fun; his eyes lower and it seems he'll never look up again; testosterone starts to make its presence felt and his interests are inextricably linked to bodily functions; the blood coursing through his body starts to flow downwards and very little makes its way back up again. Suddenly, and with almost no warning, the cute boy has been transformed into a monosyllabic grunter.

'How was school?'

'Good.'

'Anything interesting happen?'

'Nah.'

'Did you learn anything?'

'Nah, just boring stuff.'

'Anything happen I need to know about?'

'Nah.'

The polite, cherubic boy full of hope and promise who entered the school two years ago has mutated into a barely recognisable being. It's best to assume that common sense has vacated the building and isn't going to be back for a while. He's now ten feet tall and bulletproof, and every adult he knows (and every senior boy at school) is either a control freak, a loser, a wanker or a dork — or maybe all four. There's nothing you can tell him that has any relevance to his life; the only information he now willingly takes in comes from his peers. He has the most amazing brain starting to develop, but at the same time he's also developing an extraordinary ability to filter everything that comes down from the adults above him. If, as an adult, you give him one piece of information that he knows or can prove to be wrong, for this next period of his life every piece of information that drops out of your mouth is rubbish and you're not to be trusted.

So when an alcohol and drug educator stands in front of him and says, 'If you drink six cans of beer in an hour you're going to do yourself serious damage', and he's sitting there thinking he drank ten cans in half an hour last Saturday and he's still breathing, the conclusion he draws is that this is just more adult bullshit. As for the educator telling him that when he's 35 there'll be consequences for having given his body a hard time when he was 15, forget it. He's working with extreme diligence to stay in the moment and it's all he can do to think about next weekend. The idea of considering what his life will be like when he's 35, or even when he's 20, is just too big to contemplate. And there's no good reason to do so. It's the present he's concerned with, the present that's occupying his attention, and his prime aim is to turn it into a time of fun.

He's become like a six-year-old boy who wants to take the back off a clock and find out how it works — only now he's not playing with clocks. This is his most dangerous year; this is the time when he's most at risk, both to the rest of the world and to himself. He tips a bottle of whisky down his throat with enthusiasm, his main aim being to see how far he can projectile vomit and whether he can vomit further than his mate, who's just done the same thing. For him it's a science project, nothing to do with reality, and he's fascinated. 'I can drink a bottle of whisky in this amount of time and then projectile vomit that far. My mate can only get it to there. That's interesting. Let's try that again.'

At this time in his life the best thing we can do for him is to provide him with real information, to meet him head-on in his belligerent belief that he knows everything and to take every opportunity that comes our way to remind him as gently as possible that in fact he doesn't. We don't need to work to destroy him; we just need to hold on to our sense that we do actually know a thing or two as a result of our life experiences.

The greatest gift you can give a boy at this stage of his development is not to attempt to provide him with information he hasn't asked for, but when he does come to you with information he has gleaned and is convinced is right because it suits whatever argument he's running, to step right into the discussion with him. Tell him what you know to be the truth for you and hold on to your adult wisdom, even though the going will inevitably get rough owing to his entrenched belief that your views are based on your ever-present desire to ruin his fun.

It's important to remember, as you enter a debate with a Year 9 boy, that there's a strong chance you're going to lose. He's a very skilled debater when the aim is to validate his position — why he should be allowed to go to the party, why school sucks and the detention was unfair — and in the months since the testosterone began to flow in earnest he's developed a real ability to pick out the facts that support his argument, the pieces that are relevant to him, and discard the rest.

Let me give you an example of a typical debate with a group of Year 9 boys. Whenever I wandered towards the issue of alcohol and drug use, it was common for boys at this level to want to debate the merits of cannabis versus alcohol and why it should be legalised.

'OK, you reckon cannabis is better than alcohol. Tell me why.'

'Oh cannabis is much better for you, Miss.'

'Really, how's that?'

'It mellows you out. Alcohol makes you aggro and gets you into trouble.'

And from another boy: 'Anyway the pigs smoke it, teachers smoke it — they're all hypocrites. How come everyone else is allowed to smoke it except us?'

Having been drawn into the argument, I decided to do the adult thing and begin to explain the facts as I understand them — THC, fatty tissue around the brain, alcohol clears your system in 24 hours but cannabis is still there six weeks later, it dissolves your dreams, it makes kids too lazy to get out of their own way . . . At that point I stopped and looked around the room. It was obvious there wasn't the slightest bit of interest in what I was saying. I could see my words rolling out of my mouth, sliding across the top of their heads and dropping out the back window. They weren't even registering with the boys in front of me.

I paused, thought about whether I could be sued and decided to take a risk.

'OK, guys, there's actually just one reason why you shouldn't smoke dope.'

'Yeah, what's that?'

'Because it fucks your head. It won't fuck it as badly when you're 23, but it's fucking it now because of everything else that's going on in your body at this stage of your development, so I suggest you cut it out.'

In that moment they came right into the conversation. They weren't there long — it was a fleeting moment of connection — but they were there. I don't imagine for a minute I had put them all off smoking marijuana, but at least I appeared to have got them thinking.

In the true style of Year 9 boys, the conversation on this particular topic didn't stop at that point. One boy down the back of the classroom looked up, grinned at his mate sitting next to him and said, 'Hey, Miss, you've forgotten one thing.'

'Really, what's that?'

'Dope makes you really good in bed.'

The noise in the classroom escalated as the boys enjoyed the idea that I might have been caught out. But experience as a prison officer does prepare you for most things, so I just smiled at him as I held his gaze and said, 'Actually, I've got some news for you.'

'Yeah, what's that?'

'Take some advice from an older woman. Dope makes you *think* you're really good in bed.'

The look on his face was a treat and I wondered just for a moment what thought might wander across his mind the next time he picked up a joint.

My advice with regard to Year 9 boys: don't go looking for debate with them, but if it appears in front of you, have the conversation. If you're a teacher, you'll probably have to moderate your language slightly — you won't have the freedom I had in the project — but go as far with them as you can, watching all the time to check that they can cope. Year 9 boys want us to come into their territory and explain the world as we see it, but only when we're invited — and they invite us with their confrontational comments. They're testing us and we need to show courage — moral courage — in meeting them where they've asked to meet us.

So, going back to our metaphorical room, how will it be different now that it has to accommodate a Year 9 boy? It will look exactly the same as it did for Years 7 and 8, but now, instead of a small electric current, we need to run the national grid through the boundary. He can feel his strength growing, he thinks he has the world sorted, he considers he is the master of his own destiny and, left to his own devices, he will go over the boundary and out into the world that waits beyond, a world he's actually not ready for. The important thing the adults in his life need to stay focused on is that although he's beginning to look like an adult, he's still just a boy and any impression he gives that he has and is using common sense is an illusion. It will return, but trust me when I say there's not an ounce of common sense operating in his brain at this point and in an attempt to keep him safe and on track parents and teachers must hold hands and work together. He needs to be kept in the middle of the room well away from the boundaries. And this is actually exactly what he wants you to do.

He might be as belligerent as hell and spend a great deal of time at this stage pushing fiercely against the boundary (or launching himself headlong at it), but he does know his limitations and he wants to be kept safe. He won't articulate that fact, he can't, and when I talk later about intuition, I'll explain just why, in my view, he has become monosyllabic, but he does want the national grid running through the boundary. He wants to know, at some level, that it's what will keep him safe and that it's proof of the love people have for him.

In real terms the increased level of electric current is overt reinforcement of boundaries, swift implementation of consequences and making sure there's a limit to the amount of debate about breaking the rules. He'll expend considerable energy trying to work out new reasons why he shouldn't be held accountable for his behaviour: don't give him too much ground in this regard.

After I'd been involved in the project for a while, one teacher looked at me and said, 'I spend a lot of time trying to work out how to get a better relationship with my Year 9 students.' I laughed and said, 'I wouldn't bother. If you get a relationship it's a bonus, but don't spend any energy trying to get one — just teach them. Imagine that you start the year with a Year 9 class with 3500 seeds in your hand for each boy in the class, and throughout the year you're going to throw the seeds at them. If you get to the end of the year and just one of those 3500 seeds has lodged in his brain tissue, you've been very successful.'

A boy at this stage doesn't want to be caught up in life's complications. He wants things to be simple. Looking back, I realise now that when my son was at this stage in his development, I thought he was going to be there forever and I wondered how on earth I was going to find the energy to cope. I decided that rather than risk him staying there, it was my job to pull him out and I spent a great deal of time with my hands clasping the top of his arms trying to pull him forward, explaining to him in incredible detail the possible consequences of the behaviour he was or wasn't exhibiting. Now I know that he isn't going to be in this phase forever. Coping with him at this point is about waiting, about letting him go through the stage at his own pace, and above all else about keeping him corralled while he does.

In one discussion with parents about the management of Year 9 boys, one mother looked at me and said, 'I can tell him he's not going to the party, but in reality I can't stop him. If I send him to his room, the chances are he'll climb out the window and go anyway.' My response was to confirm that she was probably right but just to make sure he did it only once. 'Every boy I know,' I told her, 'even the worst of them, has at least one thing in his life he loves. You're his mother; you're the person who knows him best at this point in his life. If you don't already know what the thing he loves most is, and I suspect you do, find out what it is and take it off him. And join forces. When he says, "How come I got the mother from hell? Everyone else's mothers are letting them go to the party", make sure you can say, "No they're not, I've just rung them all and no one's going." Or "We've all agreed you can all go until 11.30 and then we're all coming to pick you up."'

This is about guerrilla warfare; this is about parents joining forces with one another and about parents joining forces with teachers. We need to learn to hold him steady and we need to encourage one another in our attempts to do so. In today's world in many ways we're letting him go, thinking he's a grown-up, but he's not, and he's dangerous, to others but more especially to himself. He's gorgeous and he's highly intuitive and the time will soon come when we can let him go and watch him grow, but at this stage in his development we must understand how much he needs the boundary, how much he needs us to turn on the national grid.

One Year 9 boy described arguing with his mother about a party, with some of his mates standing around.

'I want to go.'

'Well, you're not going.'

'Oh, you're not fair, everyone else is allowed to go.'

'You're not going.'

'How come I've got the mother from hell? Why won't you let me go?'

She just held the line, and in the end he turned away angry.

When I asked him, 'What did you do next?' he said, 'As I turned away and once my mates couldn't see my face, I smiled. I didn't want to go to the party, but I needed Mum to hold the line for me in front of my mates, so I could say it was her — it was her fault.'

Year 10

And so Year 9 comes to an end eventually and with some relief for all concerned (except perhaps the teachers who will have another class next year — in my opinion, staff working with Year 9 boys deserve special medals). But for those of us able to focus on the next stage of development, we can now see the man beginning to emerge. They are brief glimpses, but very welcome nonetheless. Occasionally, completely unprompted, you'll get a sentence from him that has as many as five words in it and you can enjoy a quiet moment of celebration. As a word of warning to mothers, when the five-word sentence comes, don't turn and face him with a look of excitement. If you do that it will be quite some time before you get another one.

Now that he's a Year 10 student, life has become a little more serious, but there's still plenty of time to play. He will work for short periods on the idea of being a man, but at regular intervals will invariably and with considerable enthusiasm go back to being a boy. In terms of our image, the metaphorical room, nothing changes at this point. Although he doesn't wander across to the boundary as much any more and generally makes no attempt to get over it, the national grid should be kept running and at the same wattage. Its role at this point is not to keep him in; it's to reassure him. If you were to turn it off at this point he would get frightened: he's grown used to the hum now and silence would scare him, telling him that he's now stuck on the pathway to manhood and can't get off. He knows time is passing and he'll soon have to think about leaving school and making some choices for himself, but at this stage his plea is 'not yet, there are more games to be played, more fun to be had'. The hum reassures him that there *is* in fact time for more games, more fun. And some boys may still make the occasional dash for the boundary in moments of madness so for them the national grid has not yet outlived its usefulness or applicability.

Year 11

In Year 11 the electric current can safely be switched off as the maturation process is now fully under way. He's still a pretty relaxed sort of dude, he still lives very much in the moment and takes advantage of any opportunity to play, but he's also starting to show definite signs that common sense is on its way back. He'll spend significant parts of this year walking over to sit up on the boundary, looking out over the side, considering his options. After deliberating a while, he'll then get down, return to the middle of the room and set about playing another game. He moves constantly between the gateway from boyhood and the gateway into manhood, and as he moves back and forth he looks for every opportunity to hold on to the idea that he's still just a boy, not yet committed to taking life too seriously. He knows the moment is approaching when the world will come to meet him and he wants to defer it as long as possible.

Year 12

When a boy walks into school as a Year 12 student, it's as if he immediately looks up and, seeing no one above him, says to himself, 'Oh OK, now it might be time to do something.' As I interacted with the various classrooms of boys I struggled to find some sort of explanation for the very real difference I observed between Year 11 and Year 12 students. It was as if all the synapses of their brains had finally knitted together as they entered their final year and suddenly, sitting in front of me were these gorgeous and extremely wise young men with much to teach us.

In an attempt to clarify this, I asked one group of Year 12 students to tell me what might have happened over the holidays. 'How is it you're so different from how you were last year? Did someone inject you with something over the break?' At that point one boy looked up and said somewhat nonchalantly, 'No, Miss, it's just that up until now the position has always been recoverable.' A perfect example of the inherent pragmatism of boys.

This is the point at which the boundary needs to be removed altogether and replaced by a white picket fence. There must be a number of large, clearly marked exit gates visible from wherever the boy stands in the room. This will give him plenty of time and opportunity to decide which gate he's going to use to leave the school. He'll spend Year 12 sauntering up to a gateway, looking out and pondering how it would feel to exit through this one, then wandering back to play another game. In the course of the year, he'll check out each of the gates, not hurrying in his decision about which one to use. This is the area that appears to present the greatest challenge to the boys' schools. It's a relatively new experience to consider the complete removal of the boundary which has been in place so long, and which teachers have grown used to. I could detect some trepidation at the suggestion that Year 12 boys need to be given a strong sense of the control they have over their own destiny.

> Year 10:
> they've left somewhere.
>
> Year 11:
> they've arrived somewhere.
>
> Year 12:
> they're going somewhere.
>
> *Boys' high school teacher*

During this year everything can come together as far as the school is concerned. The teachers have survived the journey and the students at this level are truly delightful young men with much to offer both the school and the wider community. The boys' schools I visited seemed to have the initial setting up of the metaphorical room and the installation of boundaries about right, but I picked up varying levels of resistance among staff to the idea that the current needed to be switched off in Year 11 and the boundary completely removed in Year 12. The teachers had managed the students quite tightly during their early years at the school, and they found it hard to consider loosening school rules and procedures to allow for the senior students' need for increased independence. As I contemplated the difficulties some schools were experiencing with this challenge, I felt it was worth remembering that many of these young men were working outside school hours and functioning as responsible adults.

As I said at the beginning of this chapter, there are boys who will sit well outside the stereotypical characteristics I've used to describe the various stages of development adolescent boys go through. That may be the case, but it remains my experience, as a result of the project, that whatever differences there might be, an adolescent boy is an adolescent boy is an adolescent boy, and there are clearly discernible benchmarks in terms of his journey towards manhood. I believe there's much to be gained from recognising the common aspects of the journey, not least the ability to live in the moment with the boys and enjoy them, knowing that it will come to an end all too soon.

✦ The central issue in the lives of adolescent boys is getting mothers off the bridge of adolescence, and fathers onto it.

✦ It's apparent to all who work with them that boys like clear boundaries.

✦ Let's turn the glass up the other way so that it's expected that most boys will stay at secondary school for six years and only some will leave early.

✦ The Year 7/8 boy is interested only in having fun and learning.

✦ The Year 9 boy is ten feet tall and bulletproof and everyone else is a loser, a wanker or a dork.

✦ Don't go looking for debate with a Year 9 boy but have the conversation if he brings the debate to you.

✦ In Year 10 life becomes a little more serious but there's still time to play.

✦ In Year 11 there are definite signs that common sense is on its way back.

✦ Year 12 boys are gorgeous, wise young men.

Chapter 5
External Forces: Alcohol, Drugs, Sport — and Girls

Having considered what may be inside the heads of adolescent boys, and given some thought as to how they make their way through their secondary school years, we should perhaps now take time to reflect on the external forces impinging on them as they move across the bridge of adolescence towards manhood. One thing I learned as a result of my discussions with both men and boys during the Good Man Project was that an integral part of being a man seems to be the need to belong to something bigger than himself, to be connected to a common good. And this means they tend to see themselves as part of a whole rather than as an individual. As one teacher put it, 'Girls are more egocentric, that is, what does this have to do with me, while boys are more about what does this have to do with us.' Given this male view of the world, adolescent boys could be vulnerable because, in the absence of an obvious common good, they go looking for one and may choose unwisely in deciding where to place their allegiance. This view may also go some way towards explaining the enormous influence that can be exerted by their peers.

As anyone lucky enough to have a teenage boy in the

house knows, peer pressure (or horizontal learning, as I prefer to describe it) is an extremely influential part of male adolescence. They move in packs; they graze the fridge and pantry with incredible ease and blow the household budget several times over as they do so, whole loaves of bread disappearing within a matter of seconds; and they seem unable or unwilling to do anything that will in any way distinguish them as being different from their mates. There are, it would seem, quite compelling reasons for them to behave this way and I'll go into those in more detail when I talk about the development of boys' sense of intuition in Chapter 7.

> 'Girls are more egocentric, that is, what does this have to do with me, while boys are more about what does this have to do with us.'

A major external force that came to the fore very early in the project was the boys' use of alcohol. If their stories were to be believed, they were drinking from a reasonably young age and in a number of settings. In the assessment of one group of Year 10 students, their drinking began when they were anywhere from nine to 11 years old and able to sneak small quantities of alcohol unnoticed at family functions. By 13 or 14 they were getting drunk on a reasonably regular basis, in some cases on alcohol bought by the parents of other boys for their sons to take to a party. But at this age the most common way of getting access to alcohol was via an older sibling or the friend of an older sibling who would buy it for them.

In a slight variation on this practice, some more enterprising lads would wait outside the liquor supply outlet until a sympathetic-looking adult came along who might be persuaded to buy booze for them. They said it never took long to find someone willing to help and it was usually a person only a few years older than them, rather than someone of their parents' generation. One particularly entrepreneurial group of students talked of paying a homeless person to buy alcohol for them, the price of such a transaction usually being around $2.

There seemed to be definite stages in the students' drinking careers as they moved through secondary school. In their own words, it was in Year 9 that the vast majority of them went through the 'drink till you vomit' phase to determine just what their limit was and to show their peers (and their older brothers) how grown up they were becoming. Once they were through that phase, usually Year 10 or, for some late bloomers, Year 11, it seemed to become a question of drinking to have fun, to be at one with their peers and to find the confidence to talk to girls.

These older students agreed that they did go out to get drunk, believing it was in this process that the fun would begin, but they claimed they no longer actively sought to drink until they could drink no more. If they happened to reach that point, it was almost entirely by accident, a by-product of seeking to have fun and going with the flow. They were articulate in their assessment of why they drank and it was interesting to note how clear they were that, once out of the 'till you vomit' stage, alcohol had no real connection to manhood. Whenever I asked directly whether the ability to drink alcohol had anything to do with being a man, the answer was almost always a resounding no.

The exception was the boy who told me that drinking was about being a man 'when I'm sitting on the couch with Dad, a can in my hand, watching a game'.

As I came to grips with the students' relationship to

alcohol, I found one of my fundamental preconceptions about young men being swept aside. I'd always believed the determination of my son and many adolescent boys like him to drink to excess as often as possible was about entry to manhood, some sort of agreed male rite of passage, which, as a woman, I knew nothing about. On the basis of what the students told me, I now believe that to be wrong. It seems to me that alcohol is much more about easing the pressures they're feeling as they leave boyhood and move towards manhood; it's about finding common ground with their peers and with girls; and above all else it's simply about having some fun.

> 'For me alcohol's the pit stop of life. When I'm feeling the pressure, I can pull into the pit stop and rest for a time while the race of life goes on around me. Then when I've rested a while and I'm ready, I can rejoin the race.'

In the words of one wonderfully articulate Year 12 student: 'I'll tell you what alcohol is, Miss. For me it's the pit stop of life. When I'm feeling the pressure, I can pull into the pit stop and rest for a time while the race of life goes on around me. Then when I've rested a while and I'm ready, I can rejoin the race.'

As adults, we may be tempted to believe the lives of adolescent boys are without pressure, that a world filled with opportunities lies at their feet. As I listened to that young man and marvelled at his ability to give me such a clear image, I realised the degree to which these boys were feeling the pressure to perform in the different areas of their lives and I began to see why many of them use alcohol as they do. We think they're cruising through life with no worries beyond where the nearest food supply is and what they might have planned for the weekend. In fact they're worrying about whether that girl really likes them, whether they've got what it takes to pass the exams that are looming. They're highly intuitive: they can see the state the world is in and they wonder about their future place in it. Owing to their overwhelming desire and inclination to live in the moment, they're unable to sort the thoughts running around in their head into any logical order and so, when it all becomes too much, which it does frequently at this stage of their lives, they turn the voices off by pouring alcohol down their throats. And given all that's happening for them, this behaviour is completely understandable.

When I asked what alcohol was about, if it wasn't to do with being a man, I got a variety of answers:

'It's about letting off steam, knowing you can get drunk and not be responsible for what you're doing.'

'It's about connecting with girls, getting the courage to talk to the really hot ones.'

'It's about letting the problems of life go for a while.'

'It's about filling in time.'

'It's about telling the truth, getting the confidence to say what you've been thinking.'

'It's about being able to live in the moment and being able to be careless.'

'Drinking makes you social and social is cool.'

These replies, and the many others I was given, all echoed the same sentiment: alcohol is the primary means by which adolescents find the courage to move out into the world waiting for them, and once they've made their way out there, it's the means by which they then take time out from that world.

One recurring theme that begs for further investigation is

the degree to which the boys linked alcohol use with having fun. It was a common occurrence to hear the words 'getting shitfaced' and 'having fun' in the same sentence, combined in a way that suggested the two can't be separated, that it is necessary to get 'shitfaced' in order to have fun. Given the culture of heavy alcohol use within most communities, I'm not convinced this is a phenomenon linked only to the behaviour of adolescent boys, but I do think there's room for a great deal more open and honest discussion on this topic with young people.

I wonder if 18 years is too low as a drinking age. At a time when adolescents are most in need of clear and explicit boundaries (the national grid) — 13-, 14-, 15-year-olds — they can and do easily rationalise that, because 18 is looming, there can't be any real harm in starting to drink now. My discussions with the students reinforced the reality that 13-, 14- and 15-year-olds aren't generally able to hold themselves steady in the face of external pressures and that when they're looking for things to hold on to, they gravitate towards very practical realities. Is it legal/is it illegal? Who's telling me that I shouldn't do it? Do they know what they're talking about? Are they walking the walk or simply talking the talk? I believe that a drinking age of 18 lessens the ability of students to hold themselves steady during the roller-coaster ride of adolescence and puts them at significantly higher levels of risk.

Although the Good Man Project was focused on the world of adolescent boys, it was occasionally possible, through discussion with the students, to get very clear glimpses into the world of adolescent girls. One of the most interesting aspects of our talks was the boys' view of the drinking habits of the girls in their peer group. I was left with the impression that adolescent girls are matching or in some cases even surpassing adolescent boys in their tendency to get extremely drunk on regular occasions. The boys talked of how quickly the girls got drunk and how they often kept drinking to a point of complete oblivion despite the risks involved in not knowing where they were or what might be happening to their bodies. Behind the bravado of these young men was a concern about the situations some of their female peers get themselves into and an awareness that a young woman who has drunk herself to the point of unconsciousness is in real danger. The idea that girls can do everything boys can do — including drinking the same amount of alcohol — seems to have taken hold in ways we could not have foreseen. There's an increasing need for upfront discussions with young women about the physical reality of their high alcohol consumption.

The boys and I also talked about their access to and use of illicit drugs. For a number of reasons, not least that I didn't want them to confess anything which might leave them vulnerable at school, I made it clear that I wasn't interested in knowing what drugs individual students might be using and always geared my questions to extract general rather than specific information, for example 'Could you, if you wanted to, gain access to cannabis/ecstasy?' I concentrated on trying to establish how available drugs were in their world rather than on who in the classroom might be using what.

As a result of these discussions, I believe we adults need to be aware that almost every illicit drug is available at any secondary school. The students indicated quite clearly that they don't have to go too far out of their way to gain access to cannabis and so-called party drugs and that the social settings in which they'd been moving since late childhood had exposed them to people who were regularly using recreational drugs. I reached the conclusion that most adolescent boys will decide whether or not to use cannabis for the first time during their initial year at secondary school. (Unfortunately any community or social worker will tell us that for some the decision comes a lot earlier than that.)

It's worth noting at this point that the hypocrisy of some adults didn't go unnoticed by the students: in terms of using illicit drugs, adults often tell them to do as they say, not as they do. The boys spoke of this double standard several times, making the point that many of the adults they were supposed to be looking up to because of their position in the community were known to be regular users of cannabis and heavy users of alcohol. Because of this the boys regarded what these adults said as nonsense, which should be ignored.

I was pleasantly surprised by what the students told me about the scale of their drug use. Most of the boys, particularly senior students, seemed to consider drug use 'not cool' or 'stupid' and often cited examples of former peers who had fallen by the wayside through drug use as the primary reason they weren't interested.

This wasn't a scientific study and the information I was given was entirely anecdotal, but the picture of a low percentage of drug users within almost every school I visited did continue to build, and gave me considerable food for thought. When I talked with the principals about this, we identified three possible contributing factors.

The first was the fact that most boys' schools have a zero tolerance approach to drug use. Any student recently caught with or under the influence of drugs had been moved out of the school and so wasn't among the boys I spoke to.

The second was the role sport plays in the lives of the boys. To quote one student, who demonstrated yet again the pragmatism of boys, 'Why would I use drugs? I can go out on Saturday night after the game, get totally off my face on alcohol and have a great time. I'll be sick on Sunday, seedy on Monday, but by Tuesday I'm ready for practice. If I go out on Saturday night and get off my face on drugs, I'll have a great time, but I'll feel crook all week and I'll probably have to miss practice.' A number of students echoed this view, all making the point that drugs have a much worse effect on sporting performance than alcohol.

The third possible contributing factor was summed up in the words of one principal: 'They cherish their place in the school and know there are other boys waiting to take it, they know the school has a zero tolerance approach to drugs and they know they'll eventually get caught.' Again we see adolescent male pragmatism at work: I like being here; if I use drugs I'll eventually get caught — others have — so it's best not to use drugs. It's not high-level thinking, just high-level pragmatism.

> 'If I go out on Saturday night and choose drugs rather than alcohol to get off my face, I'll have a great time, but I'll feel crook all week and I'll probably have to miss practice.'

It often seemed to me as I talked to both staff and students that if the schools can work at keeping the boys busy when they're most at risk of starting to experiment with drugs, in Years 7, 8 and 9, then by the time they're senior students, the message has had time to sink in. By then they've developed considerable self-esteem and a sense of purpose in terms of sport and other interests and so have mechanisms at hand to help them decide not to become involved. At this stage in their school career it was obvious that they regarded using drugs as uncool, and the culture of the school and among the boys themselves constantly reinforced this message. Whatever boys' schools are doing in the battle against drugs, they appear to be getting it right most of the time and are to be congratulated for that.

That said, it needs to be remembered that easy access to illicit drugs is a constant external force in the lives of adolescent boys. They like having fun, they like a challenge and they're forever seeking the approval of their peer group. These factors, coupled with their fear of failure and the constant sense that they're moving towards the gateway to manhood whether they want to or not, mean they'll continually be tempted by the temporary disconnection from reality drugs can offer.

Because of this, my focus is now primarily on the need to give young people a reason to say no when they're offered illicit drugs rather than on shutting down the supply. It's important that every effort is made to curb the sale of drugs to children and adolescents, but I believe we'll only make real progress when we've managed to perfect the art of linking young people to their dreams and linking those dreams to their need to refrain from exposing themselves to undue risk. Some will dismiss this as an idealistic approach, but it's one I've seen work again and again in the recovery of people from serious drug and alcohol addiction.

Now that we've looked at two potentially negative external forces affecting the lives of adolescent boys, it's perhaps time to talk about a potentially positive external force about which I learned a great deal — and completely changed my mind on — during the project. I had entered boys' schools more than a little cynical about the ubiquitous culture of sport embraced by both the teachers and the students. I didn't believe that sport sat at the core, or anywhere near it, of what boys need as they mature; I assumed it was a side issue in terms of their journey to manhood. Once again, I was proved quite wrong.

After talking with the students and watching them in their daily school lives, I now regard sport as an integral part of the journey to manhood for the vast majority of boys. The reason? Its competitive nature coupled with the sense it can give them of being a part of something bigger than themselves. The wide range of sporting opportunities to which the students had access allowed them to experience success and to develop a sense of pride. Through sport they could continue to build a positive relationship with their body and to use their high energy levels. For some boys I met during the project, sport seemed to be the only thing keeping them at school, the only thing giving their world a sense of structure and balance when nothing much else was making sense.

As I've already mentioned, I consider boys to be a lot less resilient than girls and when life hits a difficult moment, they seem much less able to cope. If, in the midst of the chaos, the student remains part of a sports team and has responsibilities and a goal to reach for, he seems able to hold himself steadier than might otherwise be the case. Sport focuses him outwards, in the first instance giving him an excuse to ignore what's happening until he can begin to make some sense of it, and then giving him the time he so desperately needs to think through the issues impinging on his life.

Two other inextricably linked external forces affecting the lives of adolescent boys, which gave rise to a great deal of laughter during our discussions, are adolescent girls and adult women. One facet of the project I haven't yet discussed was the boys' seemingly ever-present fear that they might be accused by their mates and other males of being gay. And this fear meant that they were constantly seeking ways to overtly prove their masculinity. One obvious way to prove their mates wrong, even before the accusations start flying, as they seem inevitably to do, is by the endless pursuit of adolescent girls, something to which many of them seemed to devote a great deal of time and energy.

'Who's in charge in your relationships with girls?'

'They are — the girls.'

'In all the relationships you have with girls?'

'Yes.'

'So how do you manage your relationships with them?'

'Tell them what you think they want to hear and hope it's the right answer.'

I was fascinated by the degree to which the boys believed women were in charge, both within their world and in the wider community. This attitude was clear in comments such as these: 'I pick an answer and hope it's the one she wants to hear', 'They can have sex any time they want while we have to work out whether they're up for it', 'Part of being a man is putting up with women.'

This isn't to say the students considered all their relationships with women to be negative, but many of them were clearly putting a great deal of their energy into placating the women and girls in their lives, in order to keep their world manageable.

Almost all boys I spoke to mentioned close female friends within their immediate peer group, often referred to as 'chick-mates'. The discussion about how a girl became a chick-mate, given that the students had previously agreed they viewed all girls of their age as potential sexual conquests, was always entertaining, the most common explanation being 'she said no'. Again, boys saw girls as the ones who called the shots: he asked, she said no and thus the parameters of their friendship were defined.

> 'Is it true that you look at every girl as a potential sexual partner?'
>
> 'Pretty much.'
>
> 'How is it then that you have chick-mates?'
>
> 'They said no.'

Students at all levels in the schools I visited talked of the freedom not having girls on the campus gave them. In fact they saw not having to concern themselves with appearance as the major benefit of being at a boys' school: in their words, it 'lessened the pressure'.

They often spoke of not wanting to appear a fool in front of girls, which meant they tended not to speak in their presence. And, as we've seen, alcohol came in here: many boys said they drank to gain the necessary confidence to talk to girls. Almost all the Year 7, 8 and 9 students I spoke to felt that having girls in their classes would make them much less willing to take part in discussions and that their behaviour would 'tone down' and become less boisterous. There it is again: the girls calling the shots.

This belief that women were in charge extended to the adult women in the boys' lives. They regularly told me that female teachers needed to be placated about things their male teachers didn't consider important and referred to all women 'sweating the small stuff' and requiring negotiation. They gave clear examples of how they managed the flow of information to their mothers in order to make their own lives less stressful (I'll discuss this in more detail later) and often evaluated the value of a relationship with a girl in the context of just how much effort was required to keep her happy. I was often intrigued by the degree to which even the junior students had developed this view of women, wondering how it had happened so early in their lives. However they learn it, as I listened to boys (of all ages) describe their relationships with women and how they manage them, I often felt as if I was watching an extremely skilled public relations firm in action.

+ Adolescent boys are drinking alcohol from a reasonably young age and in a number of settings.

+ Alcohol is about easing the pressure of moving towards manhood, about finding common ground with their peers and girls and simply about having fun.

+ The legal drinking age of 18 puts adolescent boys at significantly higher levels of risk.

+ Adolescent girls are matching or even surpassing adolescent boys in the tendency to sometimes get extremely drunk.

✦ Adults need to be aware that almost every illicit drug is available at any secondary school.

✦ With regard to drugs, the hypocrisy of adults doesn't go unnoticed.

✦ Keeping boys busy in Years 7, 8 and 9 allows time for the anti-drug message to sink in.

✦ Sport is an integral part of the journey to manhood for the vast majority of boys.

✦ Most boys believe that women are in charge.

DIARIES

Girl
Monday 17 November 2003
Saw John in the evening and he was acting really strangely. I went shopping in the afternoon with the girls and I did turn up a bit late so I thought it might be that.

The bar was really crowded and loud so I suggested we go somewhere quieter to talk. He was still very subdued and distracted so I suggested we go somewhere nice to eat. All through dinner he just didn't seem himself; he hardly laughed and didn't seem to be paying attention to me or to what I was saying.

I just knew that something was wrong.

He dropped me back home. I wondered if he was going to come in; he hesitated, but followed. I asked him again if there was something the matter but he just half shook his head and turned the television on.

After about 10 minutes of silence, I said I was going to bed. I put my arms around him and told him that I loved him deeply. He just gave a sigh, and a sad sort of smile. He didn't follow me up, but later he did, and I was surprised when we made love. He still seemed distant and a bit cold, and I started to think that he was going to leave me, and that he had found someone else.

I cried myself to sleep . . .

Boy
Monday 17 November 2003
The Wallabies lost to New Zealand. Had sex though.

Chapter 6
Adolescent Pragmatism:
Why They Do What They Do

We've taken a detailed look at what can make raising and coping with adolescent boys a challenging and sometimes very frustrating process. Now it's time to look at the surprises the Good Man Project delivered, the gifts and talents contained within these young men that I hadn't known were there and that I came to delight in: their pragmatism, their intuition and, in the case of Year 12 students, their extraordinary wisdom.

Had I known when I was on the bridge of adolescence with my son what I know now about these special qualities of adolescent boys, I strongly suspect the journey we were on together would have been significantly smoother and more enjoyable for both of us. Having this knowledge won't take away all the concerns adolescent boys generate or totally remove the difficult moments as a Year 9 boy pushes against the boundaries with absolute determination. For me, though, as my awareness grew during the project, this knowledge gave a shape to what was happening in the lives of the boys, a shape I now strongly believe can help us to make clear decisions about getting them safely over the bridge and onto the other side, while retaining our own sanity.

Let's talk first about their pragmatism. I had no sense of this before undertaking the project, but once I got an inkling of the pragmatic way in which boys decide what to do and when to do it, I began to see it everywhere, in the lives of both boys and adult men.

How did I first stumble on the pragmatism? I was interested in the reasons the boys were at single-sex schools and wanted to know whether they'd made a conscious choice to be there rather than at a co-ed school, so early on in the project I began to ask, as an opening question, 'So, why are you here at a boys' school?'

'Cos my mum said.' (It was almost always Mum, not Dad.)

'How many of you would like to be at a co-ed school?'

Almost all the hands in the room went up.

'What would be good about a co-ed school?'

'Duh, girls!'

'Yes, I realise it's about girls, but what about girls? What would be good about being at a school with girls?' (I was hoping, pushing even, for a discussion about the challenge in the classroom or something equally deep and meaningful.)

'Something good to look at . . . I'm sick of looking at him.' This was said looking sideways at his mate.

'So it's just about having something good to look at?'

'Yeah.'

'OK, you're going to go home tonight and your parents are going to say you can now go to a co-ed school. Who's going?'

Three hands went up.

'Come on, guys, I'm offering you a chance to go to a co-ed school where there are girls to look at. Why aren't you going?'

'Nah, I'm here now . . . too hard.'

As I looked around the room, I swear I could see them thinking that moving would mean they'd have to pack their lockers, and it would all just be too hard. It was as if they were balancing a set of scales in their head, effort versus pay-off, and the scales weren't tipped far enough towards possible pay-off to justify the effort.

'OK, I'll make it easy for you. We'll bring the girls here. You don't have to do anything except vote. Tomorrow morning you'll come to school and the school will hold a vote about whether this school goes co-ed. Who's voting yes?'

Three hands went up, a different three.

'Come on guys, I'm making it easy for you. You don't have to actually do anything and it would mean there would be girls here on the school campus to look at. Why aren't you voting yes?'

'Where would they come from?'

Detail, they wanted detail.

'Oh I don't know, how about the girls' school just down the road?'

'Nah, they're dogs!'

'Oh, so they have to be good-looking girls?'

'Yeah.'

'So who would pick them?'

'We would.'

They were now fully involved in this discussion.

'So there'd be a selection panel and only those girls who scored seven or above out of ten would get in?'

'Yeah, works for me.'

'So some poor girl turns up and she's only a six, so you tell her to bugger off, she's ugly.'

'Yeah.'

I was wanting to discuss the philosophical issue of whether there were definite advantages to being at a single-sex versus co-educational school; they were focused on making sure that if their school environment was to change in the way I was suggesting, they could get the best-looking girls onto the campus. Pragmatism, or at least adolescent male pragmatism — what's in it for me, what's the pay-off, why should I do this?

> 'I have one beer and then I can't drive home. There's no point in calling a taxi when you've only had one beer, so I might as well keep drinking until I get completely shitfaced.'

Once I became aware of this aspect of their thought processes, I began to see examples of it everywhere. I've mentioned some already: being at a boys' school meant ten minutes extra in bed because without 'chicks to impress' there was no need to apply hair gel; having platonic girlfriends, chick-mates, because 'she said no'; choosing alcohol over drugs as the way to have fun on a Saturday night in order to make training on Tuesday. These are all extremely pragmatic decisions.

'I have one beer and then I can't drive home. There's no point in calling a taxi when you've only had one beer, so I might as well keep drinking until I get completely shitfaced.' (Getting a taxi home after having had only one beer would be a complete waste of money; there's less financial waste involved if there's a greater degree of intoxication.)

So the challenge then becomes how to use the pragmatism of adolescent boys in a way that supports their development and helps mothers in particular to stop expending energy on trying to make their sons into something they're not.

The young man who talked of choosing to use alcohol instead of drugs to 'get off my face' on a Saturday night was making a clear, pragmatic decision. We adults often talk to adolescent boys about what they need to be doing in order to be happy, healthy members of society when they are 30 or 40. He's thinking about having fun on Saturday night and making training on Tuesday, a three-day time span, and would have extreme difficulty trying to envisage what life will be like when he leaves school, let alone when he's 30. In order to connect with him and encourage and assist him to make good decisions, we need to step into his timeframe, his way of being in the world rather than trying to get him to step into ours. This young man wants to have fun *and* be at training. His sport is obviously important, and he's showing us plainly what matters to him and what we can work with to keep him safe while he's on the bridge of adolescence.

I spoke in an earlier chapter about boys always working to a last-minute deadline when getting their assignments done. How many parents use up a great deal of energy trying to cajole and/or force their sons into at least starting the assignment that's due next week? And they do this even though they know from past experience that, despite their best efforts, there'll be a flurry of activity the night before and the atmosphere in the house will take a decided turn for the worst as tempers fray and the adults ask why the work wasn't started earlier.

Most adolescent boys will do the work when the moment arrives and not before, and no amount of cajoling is likely to have any effect. Send him to his room to do it by all means, but don't expect him to be working on it. Unless he senses the time is here, or he can't find anything else to do and he's not willing to risk the consequences of leaving his room through either the door or the window, no degree of coercion will make any difference.

When he knows it's up to him and only him whether something does or doesn't get done, when he's able to link action with consequence, then he'll begin to make good decisions for himself. A classic example of this is the students who were made aware that this was the last chance in terms of their art portfolios and so galvanised themselves into action. Their pragmatism means adolescent boys have to be able to see and/or feel the consequences of doing or not doing something before it becomes real enough to matter and to motivate them. If they sense that something will 'happen anyway', if they sense that in the end their efforts won't make any real difference, they'll simply choose not to act because, in their minds, there's no reason to do so.

I believe it's worth investigating ways in which we can effectively use the pragmatism of boys. As an example, when I was talking to one group of students about assignment deadlines, they mentioned in an almost offhand way that if they had an assignment due on a Monday, they usually started work on it early on Sunday afternoon. I was immediately curious as to why they would spend available leisure time on a Sunday afternoon doing schoolwork (as opposed to cramming it in on a week night) and asked them to explain.

'You might as well.'

'What does "might as well" mean?'

'Well, you've done everything else you wanted to do:

played the game on Saturday, been out and had a good time on Saturday night, slept in on Sunday morning. Nothing much else to do, so you might as well do some schoolwork.'

So only because he has nothing much else to do, he turns his attention to the assignment that's due to be handed in the following morning. He possibly gets up to four hours' work done on it before something else grabs his attention (dinner?), as opposed to the two hours he would have achieved if it had been due on any day other than a Monday.

It might not work every time and it might be a somewhat simplistic solution from an educational perspective, but it did occur to me as I listened to the boys explain their reasoning that there may be considerable merit in having every assignment due on a Monday. Who knows what quality of work might result.

Do I believe it would be possible to get a boy to work on a Sunday afternoon on an assignment not due until the following Thursday or even the following Tuesday? No. The time span is too great and his desire and commitment to live in the moment will ensure that there will always be something better to do if the assignment isn't due on Monday. His gaze will be firmly fixed on the fact that Monday night is still available to do the required work.

There will, of course, be adolescent boys who sit outside the stereotype I'm describing, boys who do work consistently on assignments throughout the week, who are able to motivate themselves so they're not always working at the last minute. If you're the parent of one of these boys, all I can say is, 'Enjoy it.' I wasn't such a parent and during the project I couldn't help but notice that no matter what age group I was talking to, up to and including Year 11, no matter what the level of academic ability of the students in front of me, there was general and almost universal agreement that assignments are done the night before they're due.

It was true that I detected more evidence of planning and consistent work effort when talking to Year 12 boys, but this, too, was linked to their pragmatism. They realised that the time to move had arrived, that the position was no longer 'recoverable'. They were able to talk about being aware that the passing of each day brought them closer to the moment when they would be leaving school and entering the next phase of their lives. Why did they have this level of awareness? What had prompted this development in their thinking? Their pragmatism. They could look up and see there was no one above them. They were made aware every day in a very physical way that they were the senior students, that their time at the school now had a use-by date and that the time for decision-making was fast approaching. It was in the midst of this reality that their work patterns changed and they began to commit themselves to the work in front of them. Because it was now up to them and they weren't simply satisfying the demands of a nagging parent or teacher, they moved.

This is the other reason for my belief in the value of keeping boys at school for six years. It's true that a number of boys have done well and will continue to do well in life having left school at an earlier stage. This isn't about insisting that they stay no matter what. It's about recognising that something happens when a boy becomes a Year 12 student and realises that his destiny is now in his own hands. It's about him motivating himself rather than being motivated by others. There has always been someone else in charge; at this point, if the school mechanisms to support this next level of his growth are in place, he begins to take charge and miracles can happen which have a positive flow-on effect on the society this boy is about to move into.

As I draw this discussion on the pragmatism of adolescent boys to a conclusion, it's perhaps a good time to share what became the question of the project — and the ultimate pragmatic response from an adolescent boy.

'Who do you talk to about sex?'

'My mates.'

Great, I thought, no doubt there's an abundance of good information out there!

'Would you ever talk to your dad about it?'

The first time I asked this question the noise in the room was amazing. The boys were laughing so hard that they were rocking on their chairs and holding their sides, and the word 'embarrassing' was ricocheting off the walls.

'Come on, guys, why wouldn't you talk to your dad about it? It seems entirely logical to me — you're a bloke, he's a bloke . . .'

Pause.

'What would I ask him, Miss?' (There's the pragmatism again: he was into the detail, trying to work out exactly how the suggested conversation might work.)

'I don't know! What happens when? Is this normal?'

Another pause.

'Nah.'

A student at the back of the room looked up. 'You're not getting it, are you, Miss? It would be embarrassing to talk to my dad about sex.'

'No, I'm not getting it, so you're going to have to explain it to me.'

'Well, think about it, he's having sex with *my* mother.'

As his father tells him that women like this, respond to that, all the boy is capable of thinking is 'He's done that to my mother!' The student who was sharing his thoughts with me put his hand over his face at this point, saying 'Too much visual!'

'Have any of you had advice about sex from your father?'

'Yep, my dad told me to always say please.'

We adults, particularly women, think it entirely logical that a man should discuss with his adolescent son whatever he needs to know about sex. Not so. From the boy's perspective, a perspective driven by his pragmatism, it's far better to get the information he needs from someone who isn't in a sexual relationship with his mother.

And finally, let me make a comment on the pragmatism of adult men. Make no mistake — they don't lose their pragmatism once they come off the bridge of adolescence or at any point thereafter; they retain it all their lives. But if they've successfully completed the maturation process, it seems to me that the pragmatism has taken on a slightly different shape from that of adolescent boys. The challenge remains for we women to accept who the men in our lives are and to stop wasting our energy trying to make them into something they're not.

So what *is* the difference between the pragmatism of adolescent boys and that of mature adult men? The pragmatic lens through which an adolescent boy looks is very narrow and has room only for himself. The pragmatic lens through which a mature adult man looks has widened and can incorporate the idea of doing things for others, those he cares about and those for whom he feels a social responsibility. But, and it's a significant but, if he can see no reason for doing something within that framework, he won't do it, no matter what coercion comes his way.

There's no better way to illustrate this than by describing the task of putting out the household rubbish, which needs to be out for collection by 7.30 each Wednesday morning. It's his job. We women think the best idea is to sort the rubbish and put it out the night before, allowing for such possibilities as the truck coming five minutes early or the entire household sleeping in and missing the deadline. He, on the other hand, considers that getting it out there at 7.28 on the Wednesday morning is time enough and that's what he intends to do. We get increasingly agitated on the Tuesday evening when he shows no sign of doing what we'd like him to do — put it out now. Eventually we somewhat huffily gather up the rubbish and put it out ourselves, muttering as we do so about how hopeless he is and why can't he do the one thing that's actually his responsibility. We then sulk for the rest of the night.

What we need to understand is that as we gathered up the rubbish and took it out, in his brain there was a tick: 'She's just done what I expected her to do. Now I don't need to do it.' He's watched our increasing levels of agitation as the evening has worn on, knowing that eventually we'll be annoyed enough to act and he'll be saved a job.

Some women will see it as entirely appropriate that men do things according to our schedule rather than theirs, usually because they consider we 'know better', 'are better organised' or 'can multi-skill and anticipate possible problems'. Men, on the other hand, are fully aware of the possibility of the household sleeping in or the truck coming early, but, like their adolescent counterparts, they would deal with the problem if either of those things were to happen. And anyway, there could be an earthquake or a flood overnight and then it would have been a complete waste of time and effort to put the rubbish out.

What are we women to do in the face of this male pragmatism? It's simple really, and not unlike learning to walk inside the pragmatic minds of adolescent boys to get them to do what needs to be done or to keep them safe. We need to accept the reality of men rather than forever wanting to change it and them. There are two possible approaches. We can decide to leave it entirely up to him when the rubbish goes out, having agreed in adult negotiations that it will be his job, and that any consequences from not getting it out in time are his to deal with. Or we can decide that it's such a potentially stressful issue for us, given the way we view the world and what we need to feel adequately organised in our lives, that we'll put it out ourselves. Simple really.

Why should we accept men's pragmatism and not try to change them into creatures who do things our way? Because there's so much fun to be had when we let them be who they are. Because their strength and male beauty lie in their pragmatism. Because if we look beyond the frustration we feel (and we do feel it) as we try to understand the pragmatism driving their lives and their decisions, we begin to see their intuition and their wisdom and we increase the chances of our sons and our grandsons growing into good men.

✦ The challenge is how to use the pragmatism of adolescent boys in a way that supports their development and helps mothers in particular to stop expending energy on trying to make their sons into something they're not.

✦ To connect with him and encourage him in making good decisions, we need to step into his timeframe.

✦ Adolescent boys have to be able to see and/or feel the consequences of doing or not doing something before it becomes real enough to matter and to motivate them.

✦ The pragmatic lens through which an adolescent boy looks is very narrow and has room only for himself. The pragmatic lens through which a mature adult man looks can incorporate the idea of doing things for others.

✦ Women need to accept the reality of men rather than forever wanting to change it and them.

Chapter 7
Intuition and Wisdom: The Hidden Gifts

I started the Good Man Project believing that men have intuition but that they very rarely, if ever, use it. I ended the project having learnt that I was half-right. Men have intuition? Yes. They very rarely use it? No. In fact they use it all the time, and very effectively, in their everyday lives. Why didn't I see this before? Because I and other women don't immediately recognise it as intuitive behaviour. It may look different, and men may use it differently, but intuition it is — a highly developed skill that most males use with almost no conscious awareness of exactly what they're doing. It's simply part of their way of being and they seldom pause to question or analyse it.

I first became aware of these male intuitive skills in my discussions with Year 9 boys, those delightfully obnoxious know-it-alls who, in a matter of months, have been transformed from fresh-faced boys into a species of alien that has a concentration span of 30 seconds *if* the subject fits their definition of interesting, and who are unable to do any more than grunt when asked a question. Obnoxious they may be, know-it-all they may be, but it's not all bad news. There are some fairly amazing things going on below the surface (and no, I don't mean below the waist), things that have huge potential in allowing the adults in his world to believe he really will be OK.

Very early on in the project I became aware of the language of insult used by the boys. Words such as 'gay', 'queer', 'faggot' and 'homo' were clearly audible in the boys' conversations with one another and seemed to be used almost as terms of endearment. Having observed this phenomenon in a number of settings, I decided to investigate further and asked a group of Year 9 students about it. They liked my description of it being a language of insult, laughing among themselves at the idea, and confirmed that, despite using such derogatory comments, the boys they were addressing were their mates. When I asked why they always used words that make reference to homosexuality, they replied, 'Cos it's the worst thing you could be, Miss.'

I didn't want to pause at that moment to talk in any more depth about why they considered it such a negative thing to be homosexual, but opportunities to discuss this did arise at various points in the project and have left me with some thoughts which I'll share in Chapter 11.

Moving the discussion on, I asked the boys why they never said anything nice to their mates and, in true pragmatic style, one lad looked up at me and said, 'Like what, Miss?'

'Oh, I don't know . . . "You're looking good today"?'

'Oh nah, Miss, that'd be gay.'

Having failed to convince them there was merit in speaking less rudely to one another, I turned back to their use of insulting language.

'So, how do you know when you've gone too far?'

'There's usually blood involved.'

'Nah there's not, Miss,' said another while hitting the boy who'd just spoken. 'It's not like that; you just know.'

'Tell me about "just know".'

Long pause.

'Well, he goes kinda quiet . . . you expect an insult to come back and it doesn't.'

'Or he moves away . . . goes quiet.'

'Or the skin colour around his neck changes.'

At this point I re-entered the discussion, which had been meandering around the classroom. Surprised by the insight in this boy's comment, I asked him to repeat it.

'Oh you know, Miss. If someone's upset, the skin colour around their neck goes a different colour.'

These boys have entered a phase in their lives that some adults have classified as monosyllabic neo-autism and yet here was one of them talking to me about body language! From then on I began to observe their behaviour a little more closely and so came to understand, at least to some degree, the framework of men's intuition.

When a boy moves from Year 7 into Year 8 he seriously begins the journey across the bridge of adolescence and into manhood that has only been hinted at until now. He now has a reasonable grip on his environment both at school and at home and the physical changes in his body are telling him in a very obvious way that he's on his way to a new and exciting place. But he's nervous, despite all external signs to the contrary, uncertain of what's expected of him, and so he begins to seek out information. And this is when the development of the intuition he's always had begins in earnest. He's stopped automatically accepting the information being passed down from the adults in his

> 'If someone's upset, the skin colour around their neck goes a different colour.'

life, considering most of it simply a plot to ruin his fun, and has started to run his own radar through which he filters the information he gathers from his peers. His aim? To find out what it means to be a man.

His mate Dave uses that word and everyone thinks he's cool, so he stores the word in his brain to use too; Jack does something and everyone thinks he's an absolute dork, so he stores that away as something not to do. But the challenge for all boys at this stage in their development is that things can and do change really quickly, sometimes hour by hour rather than day by day. The cool word becomes a dorkish word, and the dorkish thing becomes cool. So now he's got a non-stop flow of information coming in and out, in and out. Not much of it's landing yet. Running down through the centre of his being is a beam — imagine it as a thin strip of wood — which in time will expand to incorporate the qualities he'll have as a man; just now, though, it's very narrow. As his maturation process continues, pieces of the information he's gleaning from those around him about what makes a man, and a good man at that, will attach themselves to the beam, causing it to expand. At the moment the information is just rolling relentlessly in and out and nothing is sticking. This is why he can't talk beyond the occasional monosyllabic grunt: there's so much happening on the inside that his ability to even begin formulating a question or comment beyond 'What's for tea?' is virtually non-existent.

Having gained some sense of the way in which the boys were using their intuition to manage their environment, I watched more closely and was able to see numerous examples of male intuition at work.

Boys' schools seem to create an environment in which it's safe, in an emotional sense, for the boys, regardless of age, to play. Wherever I looked out at the school campuses during interval and lunch breaks, I was able to observe boys playing and it seemed as if the games had been set up with almost no verbal communication; there was no declaring of rules, no drawing up of boundaries, no overt picking of teams. I'm sure that these things had happened as the games got under way, but they weren't done obviously as would probably have happened if girls had been involved.

Let me give you one example of male intuition at work.

It was lunchtime and four boys, Year 7 students, were playing a game on the concrete area in front of the main school building. The principal came down the stairs on his way to do something and noticed the boys. He paused and watched the game for a minute or two, working out exactly what it was the boys were doing. Having sussed it, he joined in and played with them for about five minutes before moving on. No words had been exchanged between the various parties at this point.

Three days later the principal came down the same stairs and saw what appeared to be the same group of boys playing the same game. He didn't hesitate this time because he considered he knew the game, so he stepped in and began to play. He told me later that he thought he'd been in the game about 30 seconds when he realised something different was going on: the game had evolved in some way. At the very moment that he, an adult man, realised there was something different happening, a Year 7 boy looked straight at him and said, 'Keep up, Mr B, or bugger off.'

It isn't just about boys' intuition and how boys communicate, it's also about male intuition, male communication styles. I'm now convinced that, in general, about 80 per cent of men's communication is silent and if men are communicating with other men, that ratio rises to about 90 per cent. They communicate with hand gestures, with their eyes and eyebrows, with their head, and then and only then do they speak. In complete contrast to women, they don't talk unless there's something to say.

At a conference I attended recently as a guest speaker I was sitting waiting to address a group of around 300 women. As I watched them come into the hall, I began to take note of the noise they were making. It seemed they were all talking at once. I decided to see if I could focus on just what had them so energised: perhaps they were discussing the world situation in the context of the Iraq war or maybe the political situation here at home. But no, they were talking about which chair they were going to sit in — 'Hey, Mary, let's go up the front', 'Sally, I think we should go over here', 'Has anyone seen Jude? She might want to sit with us', 'Where do you reckon you'll hear her better, up the back, or over here?', 'Are the seats allocated, do you think? Will it be all right to sit here?' The discussion continued for several minutes then gradually came to a halt as the women settled into their chairs, checking as they did so that everyone around them was happy with the seating arrangements.

There's nothing wrong with the scene I've just described and I'm not in any way condemning or judging the women for behaving as they did. No doubt I would have behaved in exactly the same way had I been a member of the audience. In highlighting this incident, I'm focusing on the comparison between how men and women act in such situations.

I'm reasonably sure I can guarantee that if 300 men were

coming into a hall in similar circumstances, there wouldn't be one conversation about which chair to sit in. If there was any conversation at all, it would be low-level, short bursts of speech and equally short responses. 'Good game last night.' 'Yeah.' 'Shane Warne seems to have hit his stride.' 'Yeah.' But if you actually watched what was going on, you'd see a lot of communication occurring. If one guy wanted another to sit next to him, he'd just nod towards a chair and raise an eyebrow and the other man would know exactly what he meant. He wouldn't speak; he wouldn't need to. He'd just sit down.

As part of the project I was lucky enough to spend some time in workshops with the principals of the various schools. It was in these that I came to understand how much silent conversation is always going on between men. We women know nothing about it; it happens around us and a great deal of the time we have no idea that it occurs. Then, when we don't hear anything being said, we try to articulate what's happening. So, when a father raises his eyebrow towards his son as a result of what he's just said or done, Mum catches the tail end of the look and says, 'Did you have to be that hard on him?' Then she turns to the boy and says, 'What your dad was really trying to say was . . . ' There was actually no need for the translation. There may be disagreement between the two parties, but the message has been received and understood. If there's more to be said, the two males will find their own way to the next part of the conversation — and the chances are high we women would miss that too.

Men are highly intuitive, and they appear to use their intuition as a communication tool with considerable success. The challenge for women is to recognise the communication that is occurring in the silence and trust it, let it be, rather than insisting that everything be openly discussed.

I've often reflected on what I might have done differently with my son during his adolescence had I known then what I now know about the power of male intuition and the way it develops. I think the answer is that I would have talked to his intuition rather than to his belligerence. Instead of going at him repeatedly using the word 'should', as I can recall doing on more than one occasion, I would have reached around behind the visual image of a sullen adolescent boy and spoken to his intuition. I could, for example, have said, 'But we both know that's not OK, don't we?' He wouldn't have hugged me and said 'Yes, Mum, we do', but I now know he would have heard me. And by doing it that way I would have been encouraging the development of his intuition and assisting him on his journey towards manhood.

The pragmatism and intuition of the boys were two big surprises of the project. The third was the discovery of the extraordinary wisdom contained within the Year 12 boys I met. When in discussions with students at this level, I was often taken aback by their ability to talk in depth and with amazing insight about some of the hard issues. I didn't have to raise the topic of youth suicide, they did, often displaying a high level of awareness of the various aspects involved, and they were more than capable of finding the words they needed to explain how the world looked to them in this regard and many others.

I'm not suggesting they had totally become mature adult men as they crossed the boundary from Year 11 into Year 12. This was definitely not the case: they were still boys at heart, taking advantage of any opportunity that arose to join in a game, play a trick on a fellow classmate or inject fun into whatever was happening. What I did see was young men who were on their way out of adolescence, who had a strong sense of the world around them and what their place in it might be, and who were willing and able to articulate their views about the subjects I was raising.

Before I go on to share some of the insights I gained from these wise creatures, I feel the need to add a word of warning. While it's true that the Year 12 student is a gorgeous and apparently mature young man moving confidently towards the end of his school career, there is a strong chance he'll take what will seem to be a backward step during his first year away from school. He may well become a moron who is focused on getting drunk and/or laid and little else. (I'm drawing here on my experience of first-year university students.) That he becomes such a creature does not make a nonsense of my description of Year 12 boys as wise and insightful young men. It's simply that in Year 12 he reaches a plateau and pauses. As he leaves school, he moves off that plateau and begins to make his way towards the next one. In the first little while, unaccustomed to the sudden and complete freedom involved, he takes a few backward steps. In time he'll become steady again — it may take a while, but it will happen. What happens as he swings away from the structure of school is all just part of the process.

When I raised the subject of emotions with students at all levels it was interesting to note how anger was the most acceptable emotion and how every other emotion seemed to be transformed into anger. It seems that fear became anger, grief became anger and sadness became anger. How, I often wondered, does this happen? Are boys receiving a message that says anger is the only valid emotion for men, or do they transform whatever emotion they're feeling into anger in order to make it more manageable? I'm not sure I yet know the answer to that question and I'm reluctant to put a female spin on any possibilities, knowing as I now do how much my view of the world differs from that of a male.

It was very common in the course of my visits to find myself at a school that was mourning the loss of a student or a recent graduate, either through suicide or death on the road. As I watched the schools grapple with this situation time and again, I became aware that the reality of death sits very close to the lives of the boys, possibly a lot closer than it did for people of my generation. A significant number of young men are taking the option of suicide or are driving themselves and their mates to death or injury on the roads and as a result adolescent boys are feeling deep and painful emotions as part of their everyday lives, even if they don't appear to be affected. It was during my discussions with Year 12 students about suicide, death and grief that the window was opened on their natural wisdom.

'Who has had someone close to them die?'

Several of them put up their hands.

'Can someone give me a visual image of the grief?'

There was no pause at all before one student looked up saying, as he cupped his hands together, 'Mine's a small hard ball.'

'And you're holding it now?'

'Yeah.'

'So it fits in your hand?'

'Yep.'

'OK, now you've got it in your hand, what do you do with it?

'I put it down here and go over there and play a game.'

'Does the game involve physical contact?'

'Yep, the harder the better.'

'So you've played the game. Now you look back towards the grief; has it changed shape?'

'No.'

'Has it got any smaller?'

'No.'

'Will anything make it smaller?'

'No.'

'Talking?'

'No!'

'So it just stays that size?'

'Yeah.'

'Permanently?'

'Time might make a difference.'

'But it will be a part of who you are forever?'

'Yep.'

The boy next to him picked up the image.

'Miss, mine's not a ball,' he said. 'I know it's a cliché but mine's a bottle — I put the grief in the bottle and screw the top down.'

'Does the bottle ever get full?'

'Yep.'

'What do you do with it?'

At this point he made as if to throw something over his shoulder.

'Does it hit someone?'

'Yeah, usually.'

Both of them, you'll notice, talked about physical contact (in one case, the harder the better) as a way of coping with grief.

Another boy then joined in. 'Mine's a bottle too, Miss, but I don't ever have to throw mine away. I've got a hole drilled in the bottom and it drips away at a pace I can cope with.'

His neighbour added, 'I've got a bottle too, Miss, and it's got one of those cords' — he was miming an intensive care drip — 'and I can move the clip as necessary to increase or lessen the flow.'

I'd been in a conversation about grief with this group of Year 12 students for only about five minutes and already we'd developed some very clear imagery for what's involved in the management of heavy emotions. The conversation continued for another ten minutes or so along these lines and the imagery just got stronger.

I've already referred to the student who, when I talked about young men committing suicide because they couldn't see their way out of the darkness in which they'd become stuck, replied that the answer to this dilemma was simple really: we just had to keep reminding boys that there will be more moments. This is where the real learning can occur for those of us involved in the lives of adolescent boys; this is the place where we can connect with the boys' natural wisdom and find the answers to the questions that worry us above all others. How do I keep him safe? How do I keep him from overdosing on drugs, from killing himself in a car, from making a stupid decision that will lead him directly to the gates of a prison? We don't have to look far: the answers to these questions sit within the heads of Year 12 boys. We simply have to find the time to ask the questions and develop our ability to hear, really hear, the answers.

But at the very time we could and should be pausing to gather this information, both for our own education and to improve our teaching and management of younger boys, including those challenging Year 9 students, the school curriculum allows almost no room for such an activity. It doesn't have to be a teaching module; in fact it shouldn't be — to turn the idea into a teaching module would be to kill it. What I'm talking about is developing our ability to have a conversation with Year 12 students whenever the opportunity presents itself. I'm suggesting 15 minutes here, 20 minutes there, posing a question about life as it looks to them, asking about such topics as sex, drugs, alcohol, manhood and relationships in the same way I did; daring to ask, listening carefully and without judgement to the answers and continually gathering a stronger sense of what the world looks like through their eyes.

+ Male intuition is a highly developed skill that most men use with almost no conscious awareness of exactly what they're doing.

+ There's so much happening on the inside for a Year 9 boy that he can't talk beyond the occasional monosyllabic grunt.

+ About 80 per cent of men's communication is silent and if men are communicating with other men, that ratio rises to about 90 per cent.

+ The challenge for women is to recognise the communication that's occurring in the silence and trust it, rather than insisting that everything be openly discussed.

✦ When in discussions with Year 12 students, I was often taken aback by their ability to talk in depth and with amazing insight about the hard issues.

✦ In his first year away from school he may well become a moron who is focused on getting drunk and/or laid and little else.

✦ Anger is the most acceptable emotion for adolescent boys. Every other emotion seems to be transformed into anger.

✦ The reality of death sits very close to the lives of the boys, possibly a lot closer than it did for people of my generation.

✦ We need to have conversations with Year 12 students whenever we can — 15 or 20 minutes here and there, asking them about such topics as sex, drugs, alcohol, manhood and relationships.

Chapter 8
Stop Making His Lunch: What Mothers Should Do

At a fathers and sons breakfast held recently at one of the schools that had participated in the Good Man Project, I gave the boys sitting alongside their dads a piece of advice. When your mother asks you what happened this morning, what was talked about, tell her that all she needs to know is that you and your dad were here together, you had breakfast and you listened to me talk for a while. OK? That's all she needs to know: I was there, Dad was there, end of story. It was men's business, your stuff. If she goes on about it a bit, trying to get you to tell her what I said, whether you said anything or your dad said anything, who else said something, just tell her she doesn't need to know. Say it again: it was men's business.

As I said that to the group in front of me, I could see the looks going between the boys and their fathers and between the men in the room, looks that if translated into words would probably have said something like, 'You've got to be kidding. The minute I get home she'll be lined up wanting to know what went on and she won't stop going on about it until I've told her what she wants to know . . . or until I've made up something that satisfies her curiosity.'

That may sound like a very harsh translation, one that makes women the bad guys. But that was exactly what the men were thinking, and not without good cause. I've talked about the good surprises of the project; well, this was another surprise, but one that wasn't quite so good — the degree to which mothers, particularly white middle-class mothers, are overly involved in the lives of their adolescent sons. I hadn't gone looking for this as part of the project. I began to have meetings with parents at the schools where I was working because the principals thought it would be a good idea to inform the mothers and fathers about the project and why the school had decided to become involved in it. The meetings were called to inform the parents, but they ended up informing me. And when the decision was made at one school to talk to men and women about their sons in separate forums, that became a regular feature of the project. At these meetings, what I've come to consider the 'real' information about parents and their roles began to flow.

I mentioned in an earlier chapter, when discussing the concept of a bridge of adolescence, that the project has left me believing that the central issue in the lives of adolescent boys seems to be how to get mothers off the bridge and fathers onto it. While the challenge for fathers is to make themselves clearly visible at the edge of the bridge, the challenge for mothers is to let go the hands of their beloved sons and to allow them to walk onto the bridge at their own pace and in the company of other males. When I explained this concept to the mothers of the students in various schools, there were definite 'aha' moments, as the women recognised their own behaviour and understood the vulnerability they'd been feeling as their sons moved, often at breakneck speed, towards the bridge. It wasn't uncommon for a mother to look at me after a presentation about the project and say with a laugh, 'I'm camped on the bridge, now tell me how to get off.'

When I talk about mothers walking onto the bridge of adolescence and spending their time up there directing traffic, I'm not talking only about other women, I'm talking about myself. I was one of those mothers and with the benefit of hindsight there are a number of things I wish I'd done differently.

Before I begin to discuss what I observed about mothers during the project, perhaps it would be a good idea to share some of my own experience as the mother of an adolescent boy.

I'm the mother of two and my son is my second child. I married young, divorced young and, as a result, raised my children as a single parent from the time they were six and four years of age. Their father lived overseas for a long period during their formative years, but I had the support of my family, his family and a wide group of friends as I brought them to adulthood.

Until he was 12, my son was gorgeous, a good-looking boy with long eyelashes and a great smile who grinned at the world and encouraged it to grin back. He had no difficulty getting the world, me included, to give him whatever he wanted, and he spent a lot of time sitting behind the protection of his sister — she worried and worked hard to be responsible; he had fun. And then he started his journey across the bridge of adolescence, an alien invaded his body and I spent the next few years wondering where my boy had gone. I had a strong sense he was going to be a good man if he did make it to adulthood, but was he going to live long enough? There seemed to be a very real possibility that he would accidentally kill himself as a result of the risk-taking behaviour he regularly indulged in, despite my best efforts to control him or, perhaps more likely, that I would kill him out of sheer frustration.

I had sent him to a boys' school in order to immerse him in a male world, thinking that this would help in teaching him how to become a good man. While I'm sure there were some calm and relatively uneventful days over the next few years, they're not the ones I remember. Looking back, it seems as if he developed a close relationship with the discipline master at the school from day two, and that he maintained that relationship for the next three and a half years, at which point I gave us both a break and finally let him leave.

What I didn't know then, but know now with absolute clarity, is that from the school's perspective I was very likely the mother from hell. I'd sent him to the school in the hope they would wrap him in positive male values and show him the pathway to manhood. Having made that decision, I then spent the next three and a half years telling them what they weren't doing for 'my boy'. What I really meant, now I'm prepared to be honest with myself, was that they weren't doing what I wanted in the way I wanted. They were doing exactly what I'd sent him to the school for — attempting to hold him steady and guide him towards manhood while educating him — and I kept interrupting the process. The discipline master is now the principal at the school and when I met him again recently, I acknowledged how hard I must have been to manage and how much I must have interfered. He looked at me in that noncommittal way men have and said, 'No, you weren't that bad really. There were others who were much worse.' This reply didn't do a lot to reassure me that I hadn't been a complete pain in the neck.

As I negotiated the journey through adolescence with my son, I spent a great deal of time thinking, 'What am I supposed to be doing with him? How am I supposed to show him how to be a good man, and what is that anyway? What are the rites of passage that take a boy from boyhood into manhood?' I wondered and worried about him, knowing that the essence of the boy was good, but that things were stepping in his way. He was a risk taker: he was constantly out there, doing things that I sensed he needed to do, and while he was doing them, I was wondering whether I would have to find the strength to bury my son. He bought a car and owned it for only 24 hours before he wrapped it around a power pole. Luckily it was a big car and neither he nor his friends, nor anyone else, was hurt in the accident, but I was frightened by his behaviour. I didn't want to turn him into a weak-willed individual dominated by his mother and always having to consider my feelings and insecurities when making decisions about his life, but I did want to keep him alive and see my gorgeous boy grow into a good man. The question was how.

Another strong influence on my thinking and my concern for my son emanated from my work experience. At the time that my son was drawing close to the bridge of adolescence and I had begun to think about the task ahead and my role as the single parent of an adolescent boy, I was a prison officer in male prisons. As I walked the wings of the prison I noticed how many of the inmates were just like my son. They were boys, boys in men's bodies, boys who weren't inherently bad, who'd been born full of magic as every child is, but who had made stupid 30-second decisions, and they, and their families, were living out the consequences. Like the young man who'd 'borrowed' his father's car, gone for a drive with his best mate in the passenger seat, decided to outrun the cops when they attempted to pull him over for exceeding the speed limit and crashed. His closest friend was dead and he was in prison for seven years for man-slaughter. He was a good boy — he'd just made a dumb choice.

To my woman's eye, it seemed that many young men were entering prison as part of some kind of quest for manhood. Unfortunately, many of the symbols of man-hood involve alcohol, violence and fast cars, and boys go after those things, thinking they're acting like men. They think it's manly to get into a car, put your foot on the accelerator and take the car up to 140 or 160 kilometres an hour. They hit a lamppost and they die, or their best mate in the passenger seat dies and they go to prison and live forever with the knowledge that their friend is dead because of them.

It's not that they wake up and think, 'Gee, I think I'll go to prison today', but they do wake up and think, 'I'm a man now, I can do this.' So they drink that alcohol, accept those drugs when they're offered, having no idea what their brain's going to get them to do when they're drunk or high and can't remember where they are. 'There must be another way,' I thought; there must be some other rites of passage I just don't know about that can and do assist boys to come to manhood in a less dangerous way.

I can still vividly recall the sense of powerlessness I felt as

I watched my son move across the bridge of adolescence. I wasn't sure what I was supposed to be doing, I wasn't sure how to draw men into his life, I wasn't sure what role I was supposed to be playing in trying to open or reopen his relationship with his father. In the end, I decided that the only thing I could do was to go up onto the bridge with him, knowing even as I did so that I shouldn't have been there.

Why shouldn't I have been there? Quite simply because he was on a journey to manhood and I wasn't a man. There are strong differences between the genders, enjoyable differences, and there are a number of moments in life when those differences need to be acknowledged and allowed for. One of those moments for women is as our sons begin the journey into adulthood.

One of the lessons I learned in this regard came on a number of occasions when I watched male teachers discipline students. I often found myself thinking that I would handle the situation better: I would explain the issues more clearly to the boy concerned, I would be gentler, I would have a stronger sense of fairness and so on. I've stopped thinking that way now; I stopped not long after observing the incident I'm about to describe.

I had walked into a principal's office not realising as I pushed the door open that a Year 10 boy was in the room. I quickly realised something had been going on that I was interrupting. There was a black cloud visible over the boy's head: he was an obviously angry young man. Sitting behind the desk was the principal, doing some work. Not quite knowing what to do next and to ease the situation I said to the boy, 'So, in a spot of bother, are we?' He grunted at me and then resumed staring at the floor. As he did so, the principal stood up, came around from behind his desk and started to move towards the boy. This kid was very angry. The principal was moving towards the boy with his hand out, and appeared to be aiming for the boy's collar, which wasn't straight. I'd been a prison officer; I'd watched what happens when you touch angry people — you usually get a smack in the mouth. So there I was, in my supreme knowledge as a woman thinking, 'This will be interesting. Touching this boy could produce quite a reaction. Why is he worrying about the boy's collar at a time like this? What does it matter that it's crooked?'

As the principal moved towards the boy with his arm extended, and while I was congratulating myself inwardly for knowing better, he said, 'Yeah, he is in a spot of bother. He nicked a cellphone — he knows he nicked it, he knows that I know he nicked it, and some time soon he's going to tell me about it.' Just as he finished speaking, his hand reached the boy's collar and he proceeded to straighten it. The principal then dropped his hand onto the boy's shoulder, saying as he did so, 'But we're going to get through this.' The boy didn't hit him. He waited about ten seconds, taking in the feeling of the older man's hand on his shoulder; then, to recover his pride, he shrugged the hand away. But for those few seconds, a younger man was told by an older man that though what he'd done wasn't OK, *he* was OK, and that there would be a way through this situation that would leave him intact. It was a stunningly skilful interaction between a man and a boy and I don't believe there's a woman on earth who could have delivered that message as effectively. This is what happens when we let men attend to men's business.

Boys are extraordinary creatures. Their intuition and their

pragmatism make them incredibly humorous, incredibly frustrating and gorgeous. Men's business at this point in the lives of boys is to guide them through adolescence. Our job is to step back, to let the men do what they do so well and to enjoy watching from the sidelines, participating occasionally, knowing that it's their time and their turn.

I have a message for mothers, a message from your sons. When I asked the boys what I could tell their mothers on their behalf, their answer was simple and very clear: 'Chill out.'

The first time I asked this question I was a little taken aback by the speed with which they answered, and responded by saying, 'OK, I'll tell them to chill out, as long as you can tell me, one, that you know they're there, and two, that you'll make sure they know the big stuff.' They looked straight back at me and said, 'Of course we know she's there, we don't need you to remind us. We know she's there and we will go to her for the big stuff, but she needs to let go of the small stuff.'

So what is the small stuff? Listen to the following conversation.

'So, what's the main difference between men and women?'

'Women sweat the small stuff.'

'Really? Like what?'

'Like what colour the room's painted, what colour nail polish you're wearing, what so and so said about so and so.'

'Who are you talking about? Your mothers, your girl-friends, your sisters . . . ?'

'Nah, all women.'

It's important to note that, as he said 'all women', he, a boy of about 15, had a look of complete resignation on his face. Is this stuff somehow absorbed through their skin when they're in the company of older men? Are there secret communication channels out there running between men and boys that we women know absolutely nothing about? How is it that a 15-year-old boy can be so resigned so early that all women sweat the small stuff? The discussion continued and I got more examples from the boys of the subjects they considered too trivial to talk about, but that women love discussing.

A student sitting down the back of the classroom had been only partially engaged in the conversation. His main preoccupation had been doodling on the pad in front of him. At this point in the conversation, he caught my eye, put down the pen he was holding and said very nonchalantly, 'Yeah, you lose a sock — she goes out and buys you five new pairs . . . and it's only a sock!'

And then there was the other young man: 'My mother wakes me up ten minutes earlier than I need to be out of bed every morning.' (Note the pragmatism —'ten minutes earlier than I need to be out of bed'. He'd calculated exactly how much time he required to get out of bed, do what's necessary and get to school on time — there wouldn't have been any spare moments in there.)

'Really? What for?'

'She wants me to get up and fold the clothes that are thrown on the spare bed in my room.'

'Do you ever get up?'

'Nah.'

'Are you ever going to get up?'

'Nah.'

This boy's mother gave herself ten minutes of angst every morning trying to turn her son into a clothes-folding adolescent — she was sweating the small stuff. In the context of what else was happening in this boy's life, what did it really matter that there were clothes thrown on the spare bed in his room? He wasn't being disrespectful to his mother or deliberately disobedient. He just couldn't see the point in wasting good sleeping time folding clothes that at some point in the next six months he was going to put on, or recycle through the laundry.

I wasn't very far into the project when I began having discussions with the various principals about the role of parents in helping the school educate their sons. It was a topic they raised. They had the impression that whereas it used to be common for parents to back the school in any decisions made in the management of their sons, especially when discipline issues were involved, the reverse was now the case. Now it's the norm for parents to assume that the school has got it wrong and has treated their son unfairly by taking whatever action they've decided on. My discussions with parents themselves have led me to go one step further. I believe there is a significant number of mothers — mothers, not fathers — who think that the school rules should apply to everyone except their son; mothers who are all too ready to step in and defend their boys no matter how obnoxious or unacceptable their behaviour. I was told a number of anecdotes that support this view and I'll share some with you. But first, let's talk about where the fathers are in all of this.

The principals told me again and again that when two parents come in for a chat because their boy's in trouble, it's the norm for the mother to do all the talking. The principal looks towards the father and it's obvious he has something to say, an opinion to offer, but she won't shut up long enough for him to actually say it. Initially I wasn't sure I totally believed the principals on this one. I thought it might be an overly prejudiced view, so decided to investigate a little further. The opportunity to do so arose when I found myself in front of a group of fathers.

'Listen, guys, I just want to check something out with you. Apparently when you and your wife are in the principal's office because your son's in a spot of bother and you've been called to the school, you're really quiet, you just don't talk.'

'No,' came the reply from one man.

'Why not?'

'Because I'll get it wrong.'

Somewhat naively, I replied, 'No, you can't get it wrong, he's your boy.'

'Oh no,' he said, looking straight at me, a now-familiar look of resignation on his face, 'I'll get it wrong . . . and I'll get a pull-through when I get home.'

As he said this, several heads in the room nodded, the men seeming to relish the fact that someone had identified a situation with which they were all very familiar.

After a bit more discussion on this topic with the men, I headed back to talk to their wives and partners and, as I did so, I found myself thinking that the views expressed by the men were probably a little unfair and would offend the women I was about to talk to. I couldn't have been more wrong.

'The guys have just told me that when they're in the principal's office with you, they don't talk because they'll get it wrong.'

One woman didn't even hesitate; she looked straight at me and without the slightest hint of the embarrassment I was expecting, she said, 'He will.'

'And he reckons he'll get a pull-through when he gets home?'

'I won't wait that long — I'll get him in the car.'

There seemed to be universal agreement with her comments and the conversation continued with one woman saying, 'I take him to parent-teacher evenings, but he just won't talk.' By this time I was thinking, 'Yes, and I think I'm beginning to see why,' so I said, 'Well, there's one possible solution.'

'What's that?'

'You could send him by himself, then he's going to have to talk.'

At that moment the entire group of intelligent, articulate middle-class women looked as if I'd just asked them to eat snake. ('No power and control issues here,' I thought to myself!)

One woman bravely put up her hand at that point and said, 'I could do that, I could send him by himself.'

'Great,' I said, 'great.'

'As long as I got a detailed list of what he talked about.'

> 'The guys have just told me that when they're in the principal's office with you, they don't talk because they'll get it wrong.'
>
> 'He will.'
>
> 'And he reckons he'll get a pull-through when he gets home?'
>
> 'I won't wait that long,' was the reply. 'I'll get him in the car.'

The point here is: actually you don't need to know. This is men's business and it's time for us to butt out. The men I talked to in the course of the project were good men, intelligent, articulate men who, having accepted the responsibility of going to the parent-teacher meeting, will willingly tell you the important stuff. You just have to accept that what he tells you is what meets his criteria of important, not yours. I'm not sure how or why we've reached the situation where many women seem to believe they need to know it all, but we appear to be there and for the sake of our boys it's time to realise that we need to change. When your son starts his journey towards manhood in earnest, it's time to lighten up and let go. Perhaps above all else it is time to trust the boy's father to find his way through the challenges now presenting themselves, helping him where you can, rather than pushing him aside on the pretext that somehow you'll be better at this.

I'm not saying this on behalf of the men I spoke to in the project. I'm not a self-appointed advocate of men. I'm saying it on behalf of the boys, because they echoed what the men told me in this regard and they're the ones the project was about: 'Mum wants to know everything. You tell her anything at all, she has a hundred more questions. It's easier to keep quiet.'

> 'If you tell your mum something voluntarily, she'll just ask a whole lot of questions. It's rude to say "Enough", so it's best just not to talk at all.'

'I came home,' one boy said, 'and told Mum I'd met a girl I liked. "Really? What colour's her hair? What does her dad do? What school does she go to?" Mum, I just met her, I'm not marrying her.'

Another boy: 'I stopped telling my mum stuff when I was about 11.'

'Really, that's pretty young. What made you do that?'

'I told her I'd had my first kiss. At the next family gathering it was obvious she'd told everyone — they were all looking at me funny. So I just stopped telling her things.'

Notice the intuition working here. You think it's OK to talk about him and what he might be up to when he's not around, but his intuition is working really well, working overtime in fact at this point, and he knows when those conversations have occurred. When you go into your boy's room and go through his wastepaper basket looking for hints about what's going on in his life, and you read a note from a girl, you think he won't know but the minute he walks into the kitchen after school it's written on your forehead in glaring lights: 'Is it serious? Is she a nice girl? Have they had sex? Should I be getting his father to talk to him?' Don't believe he can't see it: it's in your face. He doesn't need to see the obvious clues mothers sometimes leave, such as a neatly made bed and folded clothes. The intuition of boys is amazing.

A 15-year-old boy was attacked by a shark but didn't tell his mother.

'She wouldn't have been interested?'

'No, she would have been too interested.'

*Radio news item,
26 February 2005*

A number of women have talked to me with some sadness about how their sons don't talk to them as they used to, how they miss the closeness they used to share. As part of his adolescent journey, a boy will need to pull away both from his mother and from women in general while he gets his head around the changes occurring in his body and his life. It's inevitable, therefore, that there'll be some distance, some change in how he relates to you, but what the project taught me is that he withdraws further than he might otherwise do because of our behaviour — because of our overzealous interrogation, because we keep walking towards him and asking questions long after we should have stopped.

I think one of the very important roles mothers have is to continually remind their adolescent sons that they have intuition. Think of it like a muscle that you're making him exercise. Use 'I' statements: 'I don't like it when you . . .', 'I feel scared when you . . .' Let his intuition pick up the reality of what you're saying. Don't spell it out for him. Remember, he doesn't need lecturing, he needs reminding.

'If your mum stopped asking, would you go to her for the important stuff?'

'Yes. Trust that I'm okay and I'll come for help if I need it. Silence doesn't mean trouble.'

It will be his intuition that keeps him safe, keeps him from making dumb decisions, and you can help him to develop it. This is something I believe you'll do better than his father. He's testing his intuition all the time at a subconscious level, asking himself whether what he's seeing or feeling is real, whether he's right to be worried. Your role isn't to go in and drag those feelings out and name them; your role is to name your own feelings so he can find his place alongside them. You're tremendously important to him and he builds his world on the idea you're there. He just needs you to trust that he knows you're there and to pull back a little to give him the room he needs to think and breathe.

And as you pull back remember this, for it can be something to hold on to in the hard moments that will come, the moments when you show real courage and let men tend to men's business: every bit of information you push into his head before he turns 13 and the testosterone starts to move, every bit of it stays in there and will eventually re-emerge. Trust me, none of the values and principles you work to instil in him will be lost; they will appear to be lost and you'll doubt your effectiveness as a parent, but the time will come when a good man stands before you and you can take a bow.

My son is 28 now and working as a diesel fitter in a mine in Western Australia. He's turned into a good man — sometimes I think it's in spite of me rather than because of me — and he's gorgeous. In the conversations I've had with him recently I've listened to the threads of the information coming out of his mouth and realised that none of the hard work was wasted: he got it and he's kept it. He's the sort of man I hoped he would be, the sort of man he always had the potential to be. Yes, your boy's going away for a time, but he's coming back; he knows you're his mother, and he knows you're there. Trust that process, trust your intuition and trust his.

> Wellington police dog Blade is being hailed a hero again after tracking three youths for 10 kilometres through bush and farmland
>
> . . . One of the youths was found 6 metres up a pine tree and only came down after being assured Blade would not bite him. It is understood he was on a cellphone to his mother.
>
> *Dominion Post,*
> *30 July 2004*

Without question some mothers are overly involved in the lives of their adolescent sons. Some examples for you.

A Year 7 student tells the junior dean that he doesn't have any lunch.

'Why not?'

'Because my mother didn't put it in my bag.'

'I beg your pardon?'

'Well it's her job.'

Students standing within the hearing of the school office staff using the phone to make a call home to get their mother to pick them up.

'What do you mean you can't come now?'

Mothers who, according to their boys, continue to make the beds and lunches of their Year 10, 11 and 12 sons every day.

Many mothers I talked to readily acknowledged their behaviour in this regard and often showed a clear desire to act differently, but had no idea where or how to begin. Wondering just where their little boy had gone and if he would ever reappear, they were comforting themselves with the idea that as long as they prepared good wholesome food for him to take to school and kept making his bed and doing his washing, all would be well.

Given their concern about their beloved son turning into a barely recognisable adolescent and their sense of powerlessness about the changes occurring in his body and his mind, it's little wonder that many mothers end up in principals' offices defending their sons against perceived injustices. I've known that feeling of 'I can't change that, but I can change this.'

It's difficult to consider letting him feel the consequences of his actions because we often realise just how big those consequences can be. As a first step, could I ask that, if your son is now a secondary school student and you're still making his lunch, you seriously consider stopping? There's a reason for my asking this: it's a tangible, practical thing you can do to begin allowing him to learn the link between action and consequence, something he needs to learn as part of the journey to manhood. Some of you will immediately be thinking, 'But if I don't make his lunch he won't eat healthily, and he won't learn in the afternoon.' This is where adolescent male pragmatism comes in, particularly since food is involved.

You need to give him some warning: tell him the week before that there'll be no lunch on Monday and that from this point he's to make his own. He doesn't really believe you, thinks you're kidding. You're his mother, after all, and you've always made it your mission to ensure he has enough to eat. On Monday morning he gets out of bed on that carefully calculated journey he makes each day from his room to the school gate, and he's surprised to see that the lunch isn't on the bench where he expected it to be. So, there he is, kind of angry because the lunch isn't there, and now he'll be late for school if he stops to make it. He's brassed off, but he's going to need food, so guess what he does? At lunchtime he goes to the school canteen and spends his own money feeding himself. It takes him about two days, in my reckoning, before he realises, one, that it's his money he's spending, money he could be spending on the weekend, and two, that he's not as full as he was when the food came from home. And so, on day three, he calculates ten extra minutes into his morning, gets out of bed and makes his lunch. As long as you've got the food in the pantry, he'll be fine.

I'm keen on this idea because it's actually quite serious. We women aren't letting our boys learn about action and consequence because we keep interfering in the process. Some significant stories came out of the Good Man Project in this regard.

The students weren't allowed cellphones in the classroom, but one boy had one, which the teacher saw and confiscated.

The boy sauntered up at the end of the period and said, 'When can I have my phone back?' The teacher replied, 'This is Tuesday, you can have it on Friday, that's the rule.' The boy said, very calmly, 'The last time you took it my mother rang up, and you had to give it back the same day.' The teacher said, 'Oh, so you've done this before. Now you've lost it until Monday.' Guess who rang up that night demanding that the phone be returned immediately? School rules apparently applied to every other boy but hers: her implied question was, 'Why should he have to actually follow the rules?'

As a teacher drove out of the school at 3.30 p.m. he saw a boy in uniform standing outside the school property. The boy turned towards the teacher and with a belligerent look on his face raised the middle finger of his right hand. The teacher wound down the window and said, 'The dean's office, 9 o'clock tomorrow morning.' The next day the boy arrived at school carrying a letter from his mother: 'Dear Mr . . . , I don't believe you have the right to correct my son's behaviour when he's not on school property. I've instructed him not to be at the dean's office at 9 o'clock. If you want to discuss this any further, you can talk to me.' What had she just taught her son? That he's her little darling, and that with her blessing he can disrespect any adult he chooses and she'll back him.

We're not doing boys any favours when we act in this way: if they're to have any chance of a successful and enjoyable life, we have to let them feel action and consequence. Let him work out that when he's hungry he has to do something about it (you'll also be doing a favour for the woman he's going to live with sometime in the future). But more than that, let him feel the results of his decision. When we wrap our sons in cotton wool, when we step between them and the school, between them and the rest of the world, all we're really doing is excusing their appalling behaviour and ensuring they remain self-centred individuals who will forever find it difficult to accept responsibility for themselves and the decisions they're making.

I want the first decision he makes to be nothing more significant than deciding to get out of bed to make his own lunch so that he doesn't spend the day hungry. I don't want the first decision he makes to be to put his foot on an accelerator, run a red light and die. If we don't give our boys the opportunity to practise making decisions, the first ones they make will be dangerous and potentially fatal: 'Do I drink this extra bottle of scotch? Do I try the party drug I've just been offered? Do I get in that stolen car? Do I try and outrun the cops?'

Remember, he's pragmatic: as long as you keep doing it — making his lunch, making his bed, running interference for him with the school — he'll let you. But if you let him start when he's quite young, he'll get used to decision-making and will come to understand that he has to choose to get up ten minutes earlier to make his lunch so he won't go hungry, to choose not to risk losing his cellphone by taking it to school, to choose not to try the party drug because he wants to be at practice on Tuesday. I'm serious in this plea, and I make it on behalf of your son. Step back. He loves you and you love him, and he knows that. You don't have to make his lunch to prove that you're a good mother.

I talked at the beginning of this chapter about the need

for mothers to get off the bridge of adolescence and for fathers to get onto it. I made that comment as a mother who spent a lot of time up there. When I started the discussions with men and women about their different roles in the lives of their sons, I said women should stay off the bridge altogether. As the project progressed and I talked to more parents, my view modified slightly, helped to some extent by the group of mothers who, having been challenged about being up on the bridge, were adamant that they had no intention of getting off. I'd discussed the idea of the bridge with them before leaving them to talk among themselves while I went to speak to their husbands and partners. When I came back into the room, I was quickly informed that while I was gone they'd voted and the majority view was that they were staying put on the bridge. 'OK,' I replied, 'you can stay — I'll build you a clip-on lane. But please, for the sake of your boys, stop sitting in the middle. You're holding up traffic.'

In the discussions we've continued to have about the role of mothers, Salvi Gargiulo and I have agreed that if you feel you can't get right off the bridge, you must do some good things up there and make a positive contribution. The plea that comes to you from Salvi is: 'Just let go of his hand . . . please.'

Instruction manual for mums

1. Don't worry for us.

2. Let us make mistakes, be hungry, be late.

3. Chill out.

Year 7 high school student

+ Mothers, particularly white middle-class mothers, are overly involved in the lives of their adolescent sons.

+ There seemed to be a very real possibility that my son would accidentally kill himself or, perhaps more likely, that I would kill him out of sheer frustration.

+ Men's business at this point in the lives of boys is to guide them through adolescence. The women's job is to step back.

+ In the context of what else is happening in the life of an adolescent boy, does it really matter that there were clothes thrown on the spare bed in his room?

+ As part of his adolescent journey, a boy will need to pull away both from his mother and from women in general while he gets his head around the changes occurring in his body and his life.

+ It will be his intuition that keeps him safe, keeps him from making dumb decisions, and you can help him to develop it.

+ Every bit of information you push into his head before he turns 13 and the testosterone starts to move stays in there and will eventually re-emerge.

+ If your son is now a secondary school student and you're still making his lunch, please seriously consider stopping.

✦ We women aren't letting our boys learn about action and consequence because we keep interfering in the process. We must stop if they're to have any chance of a successful and enjoyable life.

✦ The first decision he makes should be nothing more significant than deciding to get out of bed to make his own lunch so that he doesn't spend the day hungry. It shouldn't and doesn't need to be deciding to put his foot on the accelerator, running a red light and dying.

Chapter 9
When His Father Isn't There: The Single Mother's Journey

For a number of women reading this book, those who are raising their sons without direct input from the boys' fathers, the previous chapter won't have been much help. You'll be thinking, 'It's all very well talking about women taking a step back from the bridge of adolescence and creating the space for men to step forward and become more involved, but what if his dad isn't there? What then?'

Significant numbers of women are raising their sons without the direct and ongoing support of fathers and similar numbers are probably raising their sons with the help of another man, who willingly or unwillingly takes the role of the boy's stepfather. In the latter case there's endless potential for conflict and I'll talk about some of those issues in the next chapter. For now I want to focus on what steps women raising their sons alone might take to make the journey across the bridge of adolescence a little easier — for their boys and themselves.

The simple reality for an adolescent boy, which many women find hard to accept, is that he needs to know who his dad is, what sort of man he is — or was, if he's dead. I've watched many women grapple with the fact that the man they once loved enough to have this child with, they now consider a less than desirable creature, an emotional cripple or an idiot (or a combination of all three); and the last thing they want is for their son to have ongoing contact with him and risk becoming the same sort of man. There are also the women who were never in love with the boy's father, who regret they ever had the physical contact with him, but who don't regret the result. And then there are the women who wonder how to explain to their son that his father is in jail for murder, for drug dealing or for molesting children.

This is another instance where the decisions about how to proceed need to be based on our knowledge of the pragmatism and intuition of adolescent boys rather than on our female perspective.

He's pragmatic: he wants to know the facts, he wants to know whose blood flows through his veins. One way to think about it is that, having reached the point where he's attempting to take some measure of control over his life, if he's lived much or all of his existence away from his father, his first steps will be to try to put the pieces together. How did I get to be here? Did my parents once love each other? Who is my dad really? Do I matter to him? Am I like him now? Will I be like him in the future? Do I want to be like him? These are the questions that will be beginning to find their way into his head even if he can't articulate them. You, his mother, don't need to keep checking with him about whether the questions are there yet; he'll let you know, often in quite indirect ways, when they're starting to form. Your job is to be ready when they do and to show courage in responding to his need to know.

I don't believe there's a set time when this will happen.

My son was 11 when he came back quite distressed from a holiday with his father in Western Australia. The cause of the distress was the conflict he was feeling because he'd reached the point of wanting to know his father better, but didn't want to hurt me. After further discussion, I offered him the opportunity to live with his dad in Australia for a year. It was without doubt one of the hardest decisions I've ever had to make, but I knew then and know even more now, that it was the right one. He went into the Australian desert for his last primary school year and it wasn't easy for either him or me. I suspect there were more than a few nights when he cried himself to sleep and I had a permanent tear in my heart while he was gone, but it was a choice he made, and one he was fully capable of making, even at 11 years of age.

He lived with the consequences of his choice and, I'm sure, had many moments of fun and laughter as well as moments that were highly challenging. He came back with a much clearer sense of both himself and his father, something I believe has made a significant difference to who he is now. I didn't then, and still don't, know much of what went on that year, and I don't need to. It was men's business. I knew he was safe, I had enough trust in his father to know that, and that was all I needed to know. I realise not all single mothers can be sure of that and that others know their son certainly wouldn't be safe in similar circumstances. There's one thing I'd ask on behalf of the boys being raised by their mothers: Is it really concern for his safety that's stopping you from letting him spend time with his father or is it a cloak you're hiding behind for other reasons? Whatever our problems with the fathers of our sons, whatever level of justification we feel there is for our hurt, anger or grief, we have to remember that they're our issues, our feelings, not our sons'. They have to be allowed to form their own view and we have to trust them to do so.

As I keep saying, your son's pragmatic. We worry what will happen when he learns that his father didn't stick around much beyond conception point, that he's in prison for rape or murder or that he died in a car accident while driving drunk, killing another person in the process. We think he'll be traumatised by the knowledge and that it will do immense damage to his psyche, so we work to keep the knowledge away from him, telling ourselves we're doing it for his sake. I believe a better way to think about it, in light of his extreme pragmatism as he begins the journey into adolescence, is to think of it as the equivalent of a science experiment. At this stage he's not seeking to examine the deeper issues; he'll come to that in due course and when he has the maturity and wisdom to think through the wider implications of the knowledge he now has about his father. He'll pursue the truth until he's sure it's the truth rather than just your version of the truth and then he'll go back to playing a game.

I don't believe he'll ask any questions until he's ready to handle the answers and I think that, because of his high level of intuition, he already knows the answers to most of the questions he may be about to ask. In asking them, he's not so much seeking answers as confirming where the world he's been in to date, your world, and the world of his father, intersect. He's beginning to explore the practical implications of the fact he's been raised by his mother away from his father and he just wants answers, straight answers. I'm not for a moment suggesting this is easy; it isn't. But I am suggesting that it doesn't have to be as hard as some women seem to want to make it, often for their own ends and often with serious consequences for their sons.

If he doesn't get the information he needs to begin putting the pieces of his life together, he'll just go on looking, and he'll be 55, with a string of broken relationships behind him, before he has any sense that the real issue is whether his father did or didn't love him. We women need to understand that the answer to that question isn't the primary issue — it's the not knowing that matters. It's the not knowing that will make him into an angry man who uses people for his own ends, never sure of just what has left him feeling so empty inside and rendered him unable to sustain intimate relationships. In time his natural and deeply embedded pragmatism will allow him to work through the issues stirred up by either answer, but until he knows, he can't move forward.

The other thing to remember is your son's intuition. This can provide some comfort for those of you who are worried that he won't see what a hopeless case his father is — should this in fact be true. Time with his father will allow him to work it out for himself; he doesn't need your help with this. He may well come to conclusions about his father that match your opinion entirely, but whether or not you end up holding the same view, you must leave him to find out for himself. This is his journey, not yours. You knew his father as a sexual partner; he knows him as his dad.

If his father is dead, what he needs are conversations in which he hears his father's name mentioned, conversations with you and with others that allow him to get a sense of who his father was, good or bad. If his father did die in a car accident while driving drunk and did kill someone else, he needs to have those facts told to him as non-judgementally as possible . . . when he asks. Again he won't seek this information until he's ready to manage the possible answers, which he actually already knows at some level. When he's got an answer to one question, you may be inclined to keep talking to try to take advantage of the moment, but he may well react by going back to his computer game or heading outside to shoot a few hoops. Remember, he needs time to think so let him have it. Let him dictate the pace at which he moves through this process.

Whether you want it or not, you, his mother, are responsible for informing him about his father, the man with whom you conceived him. And it's incredibly important that you do it when he's ready to receive the information; that you let him dictate the pace at which he absorbs your answers; that you give him straight responses where possible, and where that's not possible because of your experiences with his father, that you're honest in identifying the bias you can't rid yourself of; and, that unless you can be sure he wouldn't be safe in his father's company, you remain open to the idea that time in his father's company is one of the key factors in getting him across the bridge of adolescence safely so that he'll grow from a gorgeous boy into a good man.

Many boys being raised by their mothers live in a female-dominated environment. Their home contains no men; their teachers are predominantly women; and their social scene is bereft of male influence. In the course of the project I was often asked by women raising boys alone what I thought they should do in the absence of good male role models to ensure their sons were exposed to what it means to be a man and encouraged in their quest to do well in whatever interested them. After giving the matter some thought, I came up with the following idea. You might like to include your son in the activity I'm about to suggest, or you might like to do it by yourself to give you a sense of just how many men there actually are, or are not, in his life.

Sit down with a piece of paper. In the middle of the paper put an X; this is your son. Around the X draw three concentric circles. In the first circle, write the names of the men your son meets on a regular basis, that is, at least once a week. In the next circle puts the names of the men he meets less often, once a month or so. In the third circle write the names of the men he meets only occasionally. Now draw a line between the various men and the X. If the relationship is a strong one, make it a dark and solid line; if it's an OK connection, use a lighter line; and if it's a tenuous relationship, go for a broken line. Now work out where his father's name belongs. If his father's dead, still include his name in whatever circle feels appropriate, but instead of drawing a line from his father's name to the X, draw the line to the name of the man most able to give your son a sense of his father. For the reasons I explained earlier, it's vital that his father's name is there.

Your task as a single mother now becomes to work out which relationships are likely to be helpful in getting your son across the bridge of adolescence and then to figure out how those relationships can be strengthened or maintained at their current level. This doesn't require you to be involved in the relationship, just to be as aware and supportive of it as you can. For example, it might be that he has a good relationship with one of your brothers, with your father and/or with his paternal grandfather. If so, it might just be a case of asking your father to take his grandson out once a fortnight on his own for a couple of hours and do something with him, perhaps fishing. You might want to think about asking your brother or your son's paternal grandfather to be the one who goes to watch him play rugby each weekend in the winter.

It might be that your son has formed a bit of a friendship with the young guy just down the road and always stops to talk to him whenever he's outside working on his car. You could make a point of saying hello to the young man next time you go past, identifying yourself as your son's mother and thus giving the contact some legitimacy rather than leaving the older boy to think this is something your son does without your knowledge or blessing.

I'm not talking about formalising the contacts your son has with older males in a major way; it isn't the formal relationships that will make the real difference. It's the informal contacts that happen in the course of an ordinary day that will count: the ten-minute conversations that happen between the other stuff of life.

This is why I'm keen on single mothers of boys approaching adolescence doing an exercise like this: there are actually more men in our sons' lives than we realise and this allows us an opportunity to check that reality out. It's important that we increase the number of male teachers in primary schools, and in kindergartens and early childhood centres, and it's possible, in some areas, to request that your son be placed in an all-male class at school or for you to choose to send him to a boys' school. Another piece of the puzzle, however, is to be as aware as possible of the resources you have at your disposal in terms of the men already in your son's life.

Had I turned my head sideways as I approached the bridge of adolescence with my son, I would have noticed some very good men, platonic friends of mine, standing just over to the side. I've no doubt that, had I asked them, they would have been more than willing to spend some time up on the bridge with my boy. Why didn't I ask? Because I didn't realise it was OK; I assumed that to ask for help would be to admit failure in the raising of my son. I'd chosen to have him, I'd chosen to leave the marriage; it was now my job to get him safely over the bridge. These were the thoughts that ran through my mind. I realise now, with the benefit of hindsight and with a new level of awareness after being involved in the Good Man Project, that to have asked for the help of these good men would have made the trip across the bridge easier for both my son and me. Perhaps most importantly, it would have allowed me to have more fun while on the bridge with him.

✦ Many women find it hard to accept, but an adolescent boy needs to know who his dad is and what sort of man he is — or was.

✦ For now he just wants to know the facts and, when given them, will handle them as objective information.

✦ If he doesn't get the information he needs to begin putting the pieces of his life together, he'll just go on looking, and he'll be 55, with a string of broken relationships behind him, before he has any sense that the real issue is whether his father did or didn't love him.

✦ This is his journey, not yours. You knew his father as a sexual partner; he knows him as his dad.

✦ Your task as a single mother is to work out which male relationships are likely to help get your son across the bridge of adolescence and then see how those relationships can be strengthened or maintained at their current level.

✦ I assumed that to ask for help would be to admit failure in the raising of my son. Asking for help from good men would have made the journey easier.

Chapter 10
Men's Business: Letting It Happen

Given that the title of the chapter written for mothers of adolescent boys includes the words 'what mothers should do', it wouldn't be unreasonable to expect that the title of this chapter, written with fathers in mind, should include the phrase 'what fathers should do'. There's a very simple reason why it doesn't: I have absolutely no intention of telling men what to do. I think enough of that has gone on already and from where I'm standing, there doesn't appear to be any sign of a let-up in the current tendency for women to tell men not only what to do but how to do it. I'm a woman. My life experience, which includes raising a son on my own and being involved in the Good Man Project, gives a certain legitimacy to suggestions I might make to other women struggling, as I did, with the raising of their adolescent sons. That's the reason, the only reason, I agreed to write this book in the first place.

All I really needed in the worst moments of the journey across the bridge of adolescence with my son, the moments when I felt there was a real possibility I would lose him, was another woman to look at me and say, 'He'll be OK.' I've written this book so other women now in that position will hear those words loudly and clearly and will then be able to relax and enjoy the journey.

So if I'm not going to tell men what to do, what am I going to do in this chapter? A number of things. I'm going to revisit the reasons for my involvement in a project looking at the definition of a good man in the 21st century when I'm a woman and I believe this is largely men's business; I'm going to tell you a few more stories about how the world looks to men, in particular the world of women; and I'm going to share what I was told by the boys I met whenever the subject of their fathers or stepfathers was raised. Some of the boys' comments in this regard were extremely acute and I think they deserve to be heard. My main intention, in straying into the world of fathers when this book is being written primarily for mothers, is to honour men — their humour, their intuition, their strength and, above all else, their maleness.

I believe men are greatly undervalued today. I'm sad that men's voices aren't heard as clearly as they should or could be, and that it seems acceptable to poke fun at men. As I've mentioned, I consider myself a feminist, I was the first woman in New Zealand to work as a prison officer in a male prison, and I can give as good as I get. There's also definite fun to be had in exchanges with men about which gender does things better. But if I change my perspective slightly from having an intellectual debate or a hard-case session with one of my male contemporaries towards the world my yet-to-be conceived grandson might enter, I feel some concern about how men are perceived.

Recently a retail store in New Zealand was selling merchandise aimed at the young female market. Bags bore the words 'Made in the stupid factory where boys are made' while the slippers said 'Boys are stupid, throw rocks at them'. As I thought about the inappropriateness of this and how I would feel if I had a grandson old enough to read such things, I was also aware of the silence on the issue, knowing that had the reverse been the case — bags that called girls stupid, slippers that urged boys to throw rocks at girls — a media furore could practically have been guaranteed. It's highly likely that, in such circumstances, the government would have been asked to comment and would have done so willingly and women's-issues spokespeople would have drawn parallels and connections with the rate of domestic abuse incidents.

When concerned men drew the issue to the attention of the media, it initially got limited traction, but eventually, and thankfully, the product line was withdrawn. As the debate continued I did some radio interviews and was struck by the female interviewer who stated that, in her view, it was all just a bit of fun and that I appeared to have lost my sense of humour. Perhaps I have, on this topic at least. When I think about the young men who end their lives because they're unsure of their place in the world or because they feel unable to cope with rejection by a young woman; when articulate, intelligent, gorgeous young men tell me with absolute sincerity that they believe they came out of the womb dumber than girls or that they think there's no point in competing against a girl because she'll win anyway; when I watch the resignation on the faces of young men who are tired of seeing themselves being portrayed negatively in the media and weary of being watched by shop assistants who assume they're trouble just because they are adolescent boys — then I find it hard to discover the humour in a pair of slippers that says boys are stupid and deserve to have rocks thrown at them.

It was my time in male prisons, my experience as the single mother of an adolescent boy and my perception of the increasing social dislocation of men that sat behind my initial conversations with Salvi Gargiulo about the world of boys' schools, and it was these factors that pushed me to consider being involved in the Good Man Project. I've spoken already about the potential conflict inherent in a woman spending time in boys' schools discussing the concept of a good man and what might constitute legitimate and effective male rites of passage. But I decided that my experience could prove a distinct advantage. The principals agreed that the lens I'd be looking through would allow me to see things they don't see, not because they aren't there, but because they're things that men take for granted.

I don't think you men necessarily know how intuitive you are or how that intuition manifests itself in your daily lives, or that you could explain easily how you communicate with one another so effectively, yet so silently. It's just what you do. You've always done it and you'll continue to do it and to a large extent there's no need for explanation. It's women who need the explanation, who need to know that this male communication is happening even though they can't see it. In many ways, this, in a nutshell, is what the project was about and why I became involved.

And then there's the other, somewhat regrettable, reason why the principals and I decided it made good sense to have a woman involved in the project — the matter of what today's world considers acceptable and unacceptable for men to say. The media came to me, a woman, to get a view on whether those slippers were OK, suggesting that the legitimacy of their concerns depended on a female analysis.

Before I was challenged for lacking a sense of humour, the discussions I had on the topic suggested a widely held view that men should simply get over themselves and not be so sensitive.

It seems to me there's a tendency in society at the moment to assume that views expressed by women are right until proven wrong and that those expressed by men are wrong until proven right. I don't want it to be so and I was keen to take part in the Good Man Project partly to prove this idea wrong. Unfortunately the project didn't do that; rather it added considerable weight to my impression that this is exactly how things stand. As a result, the project, and this book, became focused on getting women to step back as they approach the bridge of adolescence with their sons and allow room for their fathers to come forward; to be quiet at times and note the conversations that are actually occurring between men and boys; to see the inherent beauty and strength in men when they're allowed to be themselves rather than the sort of men we think we want them to be.

This is why it was considered a good idea that a woman was involved in the Good Man Project. Can you for a minute imagine it being acceptable for a man to say what I'm saying? Any man doing so would undoubtedly be told to stop being so sensitive, to develop a sense of humour and to realise that he's not yet off the hook for the sins of the past committed by males.

As I write this, I'm recalling a comment made by one man at a fathers and sons evening held at a secondary school recently. I'd been discussing the enjoyment to be had when men become more involved in the lives of their boys and when women step back and let men interact with their sons in whatever way they consider best, including on discipline matters. I was clear that this process involved women being told firmly to butt out, something I've been doing, and I was encouraging the men present to try it for their sons' sakes, as well as their own. At this point in the discussion one father looked up at me and said in a delightfully laconic way, 'Great idea. Have you got any suggestions for how, after telling her to butt out, I cope with the three months of cold shoulder that will follow?'

The noise in the room at that point indicated that almost every man present was wondering the same thing. As it happens, I couldn't offer him any advice about dealing with the aftermath, but I did promise that I would continue to do my best to get women to see the merits in butting out. My hope was that if they heard the message from me, a woman, first, there would be less cold-shoulder treatment to cope with.

In terms of the problems men have to grapple with when trying to take more of a role in the lives of their sons, I'm reminded of comments made by one group of men when we were discussing the concept of a bridge of adolescence. (As the imagery associated with the bridge grew during the project, there were many humorous moments.) One man said to me, 'I like that idea of me being on the bridge of adolescence with my boy, but could I just ask where she would be?' The concept of the bridge was still relatively new to me at that stage so I said, 'Well, I think I'd like her to be walking alongside the bridge, with the idea of meeting you and your son at the other end.' 'Nah,' he said, 'that won't work.

> 'Have you got any suggestions for how, after telling her to butt out, I cope with the three months of cold shoulder that will follow?'

She'll be yelling instructions from the side.' At that point the guy sitting next to him said, 'Yeah, mine'd be the bloody troll under the bridge!'

I'm not suggesting there are no problems with men and their behaviour; there are and some of them are serious. Men need to stop beating their wives and killing their kids and their stepkids; men need to confront other men about selling drugs to children, about taking money that should be used to feed their children to feed their own alcohol, drug or gambling addiction; men need to stand up and be more accountable as fathers. But despite this it's also true that only some men are doing these things, only some men are being less than they could

'Well, I think I'd like her to be walking alongside the bridge, with the idea of meeting you and your son at the other end.'

'Nah, that won't work. She'll be yelling instructions from the side.'

be. There are many more good men out there, and I met a number of them during the project, striving to do the best for their families, and it's them I'm thinking of as I urge a rethink of just where our push for girls to be able to 'do anything' has taken us. Girls and women should be able to do anything, not *everything*: several times during the project, I was left believing that we women are often confusing the two. I think of a quote from one man I met — 'What most men want to do is to offer something of value and meaning to the women around them.' I think he's absolutely right.

It's important to remember that I was never going to be the one who would decide the definition of a good man in the 21st century; my definition isn't important. I was seeking the views of men and boys about what makes a good man and it's those views I'm putting up for further discussion. It doesn't matter to anyone but me what I think constitutes a good man and it doesn't matter, either, what women in general think. What's important is what men think a good man is — their ability to define it; their ability to live it; and their ability to communicate it to boys moving towards manhood.

'An "uh-oh" question is one of those that when your partner asks it, your whole body goes "uh-oh". In that moment your entire relationship's under threat . . . I know it's not logical, I'm just telling you how it is. When I get asked a question like that by my wife, I have to step back, think about the fact that she only wants to know how I feel and rejoin the conversation.'

I want to pause at this point and explain something to women, something I think they'll find useful in their day-to-day interactions with men. It's something men know about and take for granted, but which we women have very little idea about at all. It's the concept of the 'uh-oh' question.

My awareness of this started when I asked a group of Year 9 boys, 'So, what about when a girl asks you how you feel?' The boy immediately in front of me screwed up his face and said, 'I don't understand that question.' The boy sitting just behind him, 15 going on 23, said, 'Oh, I understand it, I'm just sure as hell not going to answer it.'

'Why not? If you're angry, why wouldn't you just tell her you're angry?'

'Hell no. She's going to want to know why I'm angry and she'll keep asking questions and eventually I'll get one wrong and then I'm booked!'

I couldn't quite believe my ears. Where were they getting

this stuff from? These boys were only 15 years old and yet they already had this deeply entrenched view of women wanting too much information and then 'booking' them.

Thinking I might have somehow got a rogue class of boys, I decided to do a little further research. I went into the school staffroom and spoke to a male teacher, describing what I'd just been through. He looked back at me, showing no surprise at all, nodded and said, 'Yeah, he's right, that's an "uh-oh" question.' When I asked exactly what that was I got this reply: 'It's one of those questions that when your partner asks it, your whole body goes "uh-oh". In that moment your entire relationship's under threat.'

This man appeared intelligent, articulate, emotionally literate even, so I asked, 'Are you married?'

'Yeah.'

'How long have you been married?'

'Twenty years.'

'Would you consider it a good marriage?'

'Yeah.'

'OK,' I said, 'just so I've got this right: you've been married 20 years, it's a good marriage, she asks you how you feel and your entire relationship is under threat?'

'Yeah.'

He held my gaze for a minute, then smiled and said, 'I know it's not logical, I'm just telling you how it is. When I get asked a question like that by my wife, I have to step back, think about the fact that she only wants to know how I feel and rejoin the conversation.' (And obviously be careful about his answer!)

> 'We've given girls permission to be who they are, whoever they want to be. Boys need to be given the same permission.'

I had other conversations with a range of men about this and it would seem to be a universally agreed reality. There's apparently a whole realm of 'uh-oh' questions that sits in the communication channels between men and women, particularly in their intimate relationships. These include: 'Does my bum look fat in these jeans?', 'Should my mother come and live with us?', 'Whose place will we have Christmas at this year?' and, on a Saturday, 'What do you want to do today?'

> 'Men have tunnel vision and when something's in our vision, it gets done and done properly.'

We women need to understand that generally, when we ask a man an 'uh-oh' question, he doesn't go inside himself to find the answer. It's not about what he thinks. He looks up and there are about 300 words circling his head; his job in that moment is to pick the one that will get him in the least trouble.

I've talked about the situation when two parents are called in to discuss their son with the principal and the mother does all the talking. The father obviously has something to say, but can't get it out because the mother won't stop talking long enough for him to get his thoughts organised. When I put this to a group of men, they explained that they don't speak because they're afraid of getting it wrong.

> 'Uh-oh' questions
>
> 'Does my bum look big in this?'
>
> 'Should my mother come and live with us?'

It's not OK that women are interfering in this way, wanting to know what's happening, running every aspect of their sons' existence.

It's time to let fathers into the lives of their boys, and fathers have to decide whether they're willing to step up to this role. That's a decision only you, the father, can make, but what I can do is to tell you on behalf of your sons, one, that they want you to step up, to (metaphorically) elbow their mothers aside if you have to in order to step up, and two, that they don't want you to be anyone else, any closer to Superman than you already are; they just want you to be their dad.

Whenever I asked groups of boys, 'How many of you want to be like your dad when you grow up?' initially not many hands went up. Eventually I realised it was their pragmatism getting in the way; when I asked them why not, they replied 'Because he's bald' or 'Because he's a plumber.' 'No,' I'd explain, 'I don't mean what he does, or what he looks like, I mean the sort of man he is. Now how many of you want to be like your dad?' A few more hands would go up, but still not a lot.

> 'What's the one thing about your dad you would change if you could?'
>
> 'He'd get his sense of humour back.'

I decided to phrase the question another way: 'What's the one thing about your dad you would change if you could?' Time and again the answer came: 'He'd get his sense of humour back.' Not 'He'd get a sense of humour' but 'He'd get his sense of humour *back*.' It seems to me — from a woman's perspective, looking in on the world of men — that you're great with your little fellows: you roll around on the floor, you fight, you have a lot of fun. And then the moment comes when you're not getting up off the floor unless he lets you, and in that instant a wee switch goes down in the back of the male brain, and you say to yourselves, 'OK, I need to be a proper father now.'

So you stand up ready and willing to be a proper father and meanwhile he's looking around thinking, 'I wonder where my dad went, because this grumpy old bastard sure isn't him.' One boy said it in a very insightful if incredibly sad way: 'I used to think my dad was my hero. Now he's just a bloody idiot. He keeps telling me stories about how it was in his day, and every weekend he lectures me about drink driving . . . he just doesn't know I'd never do it.'

If the boys were to be believed, it would seem many fathers are absent in the lives of their sons, if not physically then emotionally. A common theme of the conversations I had with many of the students was their lack of what they considered a real father-son relationship. Many had either no or only intermittent contact with their dads. A significant number of students had stepfathers. In some cases these appeared to be positive relationships; in others they clearly weren't.

I was surprised by the number of students living with their fathers in single-parent households and found myself wondering whether parents no longer living together are coming to recognise the merits of building a stronger father-son relationship as their boy enters adolescence. Or are mothers simply finding themselves unable to cope and placing their sons in their fathers' custody in the hope they'll be able to manage them more effectively? Whatever the reason, it's vital that, whatever the circumstances, raising a boy should, where at all possible, remain a partnership between his mother and father if he's to have a real chance of becoming a good man.

Those students whose fathers were physically present in their lives weren't always there emotionally. Often during the project I wished the fathers of the boys I was talking to could have been listening in an adjoining room in order to understand just how much their sons yearn for their attention.

Stepping onto the bridge of adolescence doesn't mean you have to learn any new skills; it simply means being in your son's life. If there's one message I'd like to get out to all fathers, it's this: no matter what he's saying or how he's behaving on the surface, your son's hanging on your every word. He's looking to you to see how a man should act and he's desperate to know that you really see him. It doesn't matter what you actually do

> 'Dad spends time with me. I like it when he does things with me and doesn't send me to ask my brother.'

together: all he wants is your time, even it's just five minutes a day. He wants you to notice him. One boy described with absolute joy and pride how his father comes in at the end of each day, sits on the edge of his bed just before he's ready to turn the light off and asks, 'How was your day?' Just a five-minute conversation each night allows that boy to know his father cares.

One boy described how his father had started the practice of asking him each night, 'So what question did you ask a teacher today?' The boy said that for the first little while, he had to ask a teacher what he or she had had for lunch, just so he had something to tell his dad. But eventually he managed to ask a question in class, and he was really excited that he would have something to impress his dad with that night.

Your boy would walk across broken glass for you; you'll be doing him a great favour if you can remember that. He wants to know that when you're talking to him you're fully present. He doesn't want you to give up work, to look after him 24 hours a day or to completely invade his world — if you were to do so, I think it would be fair to suggest you'd scare him half to death. What he does want is for you to know what his favourite food is, what music he likes, who his best friend is, what scares him and what his dreams are. He knows implicitly his mother has that information because that's what mothers do — one way or another we find out everything — but he yearns for his father to know it too.

One boy described how excited he was about a car that his mate had just bought, but when he asked his dad to come outside and have a look, the reply was, 'What for? I'm not into cars.' The boy wasn't asking his father to get excited about cars; he wanted to draw him into the world that excited him. It's not about your world; it's about his. You might wonder why he likes what he does, why he's not into the same things as you. My advice would be, just be patient. In the majority of cases he'll find his way back to the things that matter to and interest you, but much of the journey at this point is about trying to establish his own identity, and one of the tests he's setting you as he does so is whether you care enough to cross into his world.

> Men looking at their children: in their eyes concern, fierce pride, awkward tenderness.
>
> *Sara Donati,*
> *Lake in the Clouds*

He wants you to connect with him as he is now, not as

you might want him to be. Think about stepping into the moment with your boy whenever the opportunity presents itself, and it will. Be aware that the very fact you're his father makes you the right person to be there. You don't have to add any skills, you don't have to become any different from the guy you've always been. You just need to look towards your boy on a regular basis, and to think about organising your life in a way that allows you to spend some time with him.

The other thing you don't have to do is to lecture him. That 'proper father' thing seems to leave you feeling that by continuing to fool around with him, you're in some way being a negligent dad. It's as if there's now a list you consider you have to work through, giving him a lecture on each of the main topics of life — alcohol, sex, cars, and so on. Actually you don't have to give him any lectures at all. You just have to be prepared to answer any question he asks as honestly as you can when he asks it; if you need time to consider your reply, tell him that. Needing time to think is something he understands extremely well. If you do need time to think and tell him you'll get back to him, make sure you do — keeping your word is one of the main indicators of your awareness of your son.

I noted earlier that a significant number of the boys I spoke to had stepfathers, and most described their relationships with these men as a negative aspect of their lives. It's difficult being the stepfather of an adolescent boy. Even if you've been in the boy's life for a long time, as he begins his own investigation of manhood, you'll come under immense scrutiny and whenever he feels anger at being controlled in the way he needs to be as an early adolescent, he'll be comparing you with his father, who will inevitably appear the better man. Even those boys who said they had a great relationship with their stepdad, and a number went so far as to state without embarrassment that he was a great guy and they really loved him, would then say, 'but he's not my dad'.

This is perhaps the only real advice I can give those stepfathers wanting to know what they should be doing as their stepson moves towards the bridge of adolescence: whether physically or emotionally, make room for his father. If you can talk about his dad, mention him at least. In that way you're giving your stepson a chance to put the pieces together. It doesn't mean he'll love you any less— there's enough love for you both — and if you're worried about the choices he might make because of his father's influence or the reality of his life, tell him that. But tell him objectively, not in a way that implies the boy is an idiot if he gives any credence at all to his father's view of the world. You may well be the only one who can talk to him about his father in an objective way; his mother may still be immersed in the anger or hurt attached to the breakdown of the relationship. In those circumstances, you have enormous potential as a stabilising influence.

The only other comment I would make in this regard is that if you are newly on the scene in an adolescent boy's life and in a sexual relationship with his mother, go carefully. Don't for a minute assume that because you're with his mother, he has any duty or responsibility at all to respect you any more than he would any other adult. The fact that you're with his mother sets the scene for a highly charged emotional environment. In some situations he'll perceive you as having usurped his role as the man of the house.

Challenges will come. You're the adult and you're the newcomer. Go carefully with him, give him some space — a lot of space — and (this is a plea on his behalf) please don't try to become his father. If you earn his respect, he'll give it to you, but it will take time.

I'm very conscious that I started this chapter pledging not to tell fathers what to do, so I'm stepping carefully here. If you were to ask my opinion about your role as a father in the life of your adolescent son, on the basis of what the boys told me I'd answer that you should be on the bridge of adolescence to show your boy what manhood is. Your role is also to create pathways to other men, so that the stuff that he can't talk to you about, because he's so pragmatic, he can talk about to another male. Accept that he will talk to another man, because there are some things he can't talk to you about (especially if you are in a sexual relationship with his mother!). Being a good father doesn't mean that your son talks to you about absolutely everything; being a good father is simply being there. In his eyes, you're enough exactly as you are now, simply because you're his father; you're special because you're the only one he can call 'Dad'. That's all he's focused on. Continue to be who you are, continue to walk beside him and he'll be the good man he has the potential to become. And you'll both have a great deal of fun along the way.

Instruction manual for dads

1. Show an interest in what we do.

2. Ask questions.

3. Trust me.

Year 7 high school student

✦ All I really needed in the worst moments of the journey across the bridge of adolescence with my son was another woman to look at me and say, 'He'll be OK.'

✦ Men's voices aren't heard as clearly as they should or could be and it seems acceptable to poke fun at men.

✦ There's a tendency in society to assume that views expressed by women are right until proven wrong and that those expressed by men are wrong until proven right.

✦ Girls and women should be able to do anything, not *everything*. Women often confuse the two.

✦ Your sons want you to step up, elbowing their mothers aside if you need to.

✦ Your boys don't want you to be anyone else; they just want you to be their dad.

✦ The moment you can't get off the floor until he lets you, you say to yourself, 'OK, I need to be a proper father now.'

✦ Where at all possible raising a boy should be a partnership between his mother and father.

✦ All he wants is your time, even if it's just five minutes a day.

✦ He wants you to connect with him as he is now, not as you might want him to be.

✦ You don't have to give him lectures. Just answer any questions honestly and when he asks them.

✦ As your stepson moves towards the bridge of adolescence, make room for his father, physically or emotionally.

✦ Don't for a minute assume that because you're with his mother he has any duty or responsibility to respect you more than he would any other adult.

✦ Fathers must also allow their sons to talk to other men about the stuff they can't discuss with their dads.

Chapter 11
Growing a Good Man: What It Takes

And so it's time to draw together the final strands of information and consider what other steps we might take to help our gorgeous boys to grow into good men.

The Good Man Project was started in order to establish an agreed definition of a good man which could be promulgated and which would form the basis of further work to be done in boys' schools concerning rites of passage and the entry to manhood. With this aim in mind, I took every opportunity to ask the men I met and each class of boys I talked with to tell me what they thought were the top three qualities of a good man. As you can imagine, there was a wide variety of answers and the extensive list of the qualities identified appears at the end of this chapter.

To a certain degree, many of the answers were those I had expected and/or hoped for, but there was one major surprise: the top three qualities of a good man emerged as trust, loyalty and a sense of humour. I easily accepted the first two, but initially whenever a sense of humour was mentioned, I would try to dismiss the idea, considering it a nice quality to have, but not something that was an intrinsic part of being a good man. In the end, however, I was forced to concede the point, especially in light of the boys' assertion that they would, if they could, ensure their fathers got their sense of humour back. Also, as the project progressed, I could see how big a part humour plays in the lives of men. Wherever they are, humour is there too; despite their best efforts, women who want a situation to be taken seriously usually find that they're pushing against the tide. Men will do what needs to be done, they'll deal very well with serious and solemn situations, but if there's any chance at all that humour can be brought into a situation while still achieving the required outcome, they'll make sure this happens.

It wasn't long before the principals and I agreed to abandon the idea of developing a definition of a good man. It very quickly became obvious that what we were looking for was far too fluid to be set down in a few words or phrases and that trying to do so could reinforce male stereotypes that would work against our basic aim of freeing boys up to explore what makes a good man. A definition set in concrete could do more harm than good and stop ongoing examination of the concept of manhood in the 21st century.

In assessing those top three qualities of trust, loyalty and a sense of humour, it's possible to offer the argument that they're not qualities unique to men. Women can be loyal, women can be trusted and extend trust and women have a sense of humour — it's perhaps not as extensive as men's in some instances, but we do have one. So are there really differences in the attributes considered ideal qualities for good men versus good women, and if so, where do those differences lie? My thoughts on this issue are still relatively underdeveloped, but my view at the moment is that the differences lie not in the qualities themselves but in how they're manifested.

For instance, what does loyalty look like to me, a woman? Loyalty is when I ring a friend and tell her I need to talk and she makes herself available as soon as she can without stopping to ask whether the situation is really that urgent. Loyalty is about her then listening without judgement, regardless of how much of a fool I might be making of myself in the situation I'm describing. As I've mentioned, when I asked a group of boys what loyalty looked like, they said it was staying with your mates in the face of threat.

And this is where the work can begin in our attempts to keep more of our boys alive. Knowing that in their eyes loyalty is seen as part of being a man and means standing by your mates, we can perhaps understand a little better why they put their foot down on the accelerator when urged to do so by their best friends. They don't think about the risk they're taking; they think about being a man and about being loyal and they and their friends die when they wrap their cars around power poles or trees. We have to get them to understand that loyalty is keeping your mates safe; it's stopping at orange lights and staying within the speed limit.

Although I believe that the majority of the characteristics listed at the end of the chapter can be applied to both men and women, there's one that I think might be unique to men, or at least more applicable to men than women. It's the need and/or desire for men to belong to something bigger than themselves, to see themselves as part of a whole. The words given to me by the men and boys I spoke to included 'committed to', 'belonging to', 'being part of something', 'attending' and 'participating'. Men asked to consider at what point in their lives they'd become a man often talked about when their father died. A man stands linked to the past by his father, to the future by his children, and his place in the world is defined by the line that stretches between the three. So when his father dies and he's forced to a different place in the line, his world shifts and, in his own eyes, he finally becomes a man, even if he's been there for a while as far as others are concerned.

As a society I think we've been hooked for some time on the idea that the lack of highly visible positive male role models is contributing to our high rates of male suicide, imprisonment and road death. Before the Good Man Project I shared that view, but after my conversations with boys, I'm not quite so sure.

Time and again I asked the students who their role models were and who influenced their view of what makes a good man, and almost always they replied in a way that separated the men in their immediate circle from the so-called role models in the public arena. They made a very definite distinction between the men they admired and those they actually wanted to be like and were very clear in their assertions that they needed to know a man personally before they could decide whether he merited being described as a good man.

In our discussions they identified three distinct groups of men, each of whom acted as role models for them in different ways. There were the men who had access to what the students might want in later life (wealth, cars, power); the men who had achieved excellence in their particular field of interest; and the men they might actually want to be like.

In the first category they spoke of men in the public eye, usually international figures, including soccer star

David Beckham and a number of entertainers. These men were considered role models because of their wealth, the glamorous life they appeared to be living (cars and women featured heavily in the boys' assessment of the glamour factor) and the fact they were wealthy enough to always be where they wanted to be, doing what they wanted to do.

In the second category they spoke of sportsmen, including racing driver Michael Schumacher and top rugby and cricket players. It was their achievement of excellence that made the boys look up to these men: they admired their willingness to dedicate themselves to something and to stick with it.

Having identified these two categories and the difference between the two, I then went on to ask whether these men were good men. The boys invariably replied in their pragmatic way, 'Dunno, don't know them', that is, they couldn't answer that question because they had no idea what sort of people these men actually were.

That is what led me on to the third category, which I'm inclined to call heroes. These were the men they knew personally, the men they actually aspired to be like. In this group were their grandfathers, their uncles, their older brothers and their mates' older brothers, their teachers and their coaches and, on rare occasions, their fathers. It's here rather than in the public arena that we should be looking for potential positive male role models.

I understood better how the boys differentiate between men in what we might consider public role model positions and those men who actually influence their day-to-day behaviour when, sometime during the project, a prominent New Zealand cricketer appeared on the front page of a Sunday paper after having been involved in an incident in a

South African nightclub while the Black Caps were on tour. Given that I was immersed in the issues associated with adolescent boys, I felt angry on their behalf, considering it was less then helpful that a prominent sportsman should behave in that way. I might just as well have saved my energy. When I raised the matter with a group of students, expressing my view that this player had set them a bad example, they stared back at me blank-faced: they had absolutely no idea what I was getting so excited about.

As I continued to expand my thoughts about him being a poor role model and so on, they proceeded to reject every argument I offered to support my belief that his behaviour had been inappropriate — 'there were nine days until the next game', 'you can't trust what was being reported', 'if he wasn't famous, the media wouldn't be picking on him'. The boys agreed that they wouldn't want, and wouldn't be allowed, to behave in such a way while away with their school sports team because it would let their team-mates down. But this fact did nothing to undermine their belief that, despite this behaviour, this player was a good guy and that whatever had happened in the nightclub was completely irrelevant to the main issue — his ability to play a good game of cricket for his country.

I thought, and many other adults would too, that the boys would assess the player's behaviour and decide that if he could do it, so could they. For the boys I was talking to, nothing could have been further from the truth. They lived according to different expectations, their behaviour was motivated by loyalty to their mates, and they separated the behaviour of this supposed role model from the issue of whether he played well and thus represented his country honourably. Their sense of fairness was evident too. In their eyes this guy was being targeted only because he was well known and what was being reported in the media couldn't be trusted.

It was this conversation that led me to seriously question whether the supposed lack of highly visible positive male role models does contribute much at all to our negative youth statistics. Good role models are important; there can be no argument with that. Men like John Eales help to identify achievable future pathways for boys. But I now believe that the real answer to such problems as youth suicide, youth offending and imprisonment and the increasing youth road toll lies in strengthening boys' links to the good men in their immediate circle — their heroes — and in helping fathers to remain heroes and positive influences in the lives of their sons.

The answer also lies in getting ordinary men's stories into the cultural fabric of our society. During the project I spent an evening with the principals involved during which each of them spoke for five to ten minutes, sharing their stories of when they had become men. It will remain one of the most memorable nights of my life. To watch adult men reach back to find that moment and then find the words to share it with their peers was to know the strength, humour and pure delight of men when they're affirmed for being who and what they are. If men can begin to share these stories with their sons, with other men and perhaps even with their wives and partners, and if we can honour those stories within our society as they deserve to be honoured, we'll be taking a significant step forward in guiding our young men successfully across the bridge of adolescence and into manhood.

But in terms of strengthening boys' links to the good men

in their immediate circle, another dilemma presents itself. If the challenge is our ability to put heroes, good men, into the lives of boys, we're going to have to address, and soon, the matter of getting more men into teaching, and at all levels. There are a number of reasons for the dearth of male teachers at early childhood and primary level, not least the political correctness that is strangling us as a society. The solutions won't be easily found, but find them we must.

What of actual rites of passage? What is being done or might be done to allow boys to recognise that they're on their way into manhood?

All the boys' schools I visited during the Good Man Project put a considerable amount of time and effort into celebrating excellence, both at school assemblies and on a number of other occasions. The boys heard positive language about manhood as a matter of course; they were regularly exposed to conversations that affirmed the value of being male. And they could see evidence of success through effort every day in the photos and plaques on the walls and in the display cabinets of awards. It was this that made me focus on the need to provide boys with positive rites of passage rather than the potentially fatal ones of alcohol, drugs and fast cars (or a mixture of all three).

I believe the opportunities to create positive rites of passage for boys are there within the structures of both single-sex and co-ed schools. Entering the school in Year 7, moving into the senior school in Year 11 and the step from Year 11 to 12 all appear to be natural gateways that schools can highlight and use — and many boys' schools are already doing so.

The Year 7 boy needs affirmation, overt affirmation, that

when he arrives at the gate of secondary school for the first time he's moving onto the bridge of adolescence. As I've said before, his eyes are up and he's looking towards the senior students, thinking about the journey ahead. In whatever way works best, given the particular school environment, it's important to make him as aware as possible of the significance of this particular moment.

The boys themselves spoke of the impact of becoming a senior student and realising that they were moving towards manhood and greater levels of self-responsibility. To some extent, the move from the junior to the senior school is the moment when a student really decides to be part of the wider school. At this point they're in effect choosing to be at school — they no longer have to be there. Most of the Year 11 boys I talked to confirmed that this made a difference to their attitude. They agreed that going into Year 11 also meant an increased workload, though they had more choice about when and if they actually did the work required. There was general agreement, however, that the step from Year 11 to Year 12 was the big one for them, the point at which they became noticeably more in control of their own lives.

The various schools I visited marked the entry into the senior school in slightly different ways. There was often a change in uniform and senior boys often had their own space within the school and/or could leave the school grounds without having to seek permission. Prefect systems took different forms in each school, some having moved towards the idea of leaders and mentors.

The other rite of passage noticeable within boys' schools was the graduation of students from Year 12, often celebrated in great style. This rite of passage is one every school appeared to honour, with a clear sense of history and tradition that the boys obviously enjoyed.

Emotional literacy, emotional resilience, emotional confidence — these phrases were all part of the conversation when the principals and I discussed the needs of boys before the Good Man Project got under way. Emotional literacy was the phrase we were using at the start of the project, the one everyone seemed most comfortable with, but as time went on, we began to question whether this was in fact the right way to explain what they were reaching for on behalf of their students. It seemed to suggest the need to have a significant number of words on hand to describe whatever feeling a person might be experiencing. After considerable discussion, the principals decided they preferred to work with the phrase emotional confidence. That was what they wanted for their students.

What is emotional confidence? How is it different from emotional literacy? This is the definition agreed on by the principals: the ability to ask and answer reflective questions; the ability to think about the world around them and their part in it; and the ability to find the language to describe how they see that world. Focusing on emotional confidence rather than emotional literacy means not only having a number of options on hand when looking for a word to explain a feeling, but also having the freedom to decide whether talking is necessary and, if so, what needs to be said.

In my initial conversations with the students, I was struck by how many of them seemed to lack a satisfactory word bank: it wasn't that they didn't have anything to say, rather that they lacked the words to say it. The pauses, the repetition of certain well-used words, the shrugging of the shoulders if they gave a one-word response and I asked another question — all these appeared to indicate an inability to find the words (not to be mistaken for their need to pause and think before they answered).

The contrast between the sexes in this area was made very obvious when I visited a school that incorporated girls into its senior classes and spent some time with a group of girls, asking them the same sort of questions I'd asked the boys. I only had to ask the girls one or two questions and the entire time available was then filled with conversation and discussion. They required no prompting: they needed to know only the general direction I wanted for the discussion before taking control.

Some of what I was seeing was directly attributable to a basic gender difference — most women I know seem to have no difficulty (at least in men's eyes) in expressing an opinion or describing their emotions — but I came to believe that at least some of the difference I was seeing was a direct result of the boys' lack of an adequate word bank.

Often, when you ask an adolescent boy how he is or how his day has been, he'll respond with one word — 'good'. If it's his mother or perhaps even another woman asking the question, she'll tend to wait for some expansion on the concept of 'good' and if it isn't forthcoming, she'll proceed to ask several more questions until she gets what she considers to be sufficient information. (She'll often ask these follow-up questions while peering into the boy's face, thus ensuring that she'll get very little additional information.) We don't need to expand the word bank of adolescent boys so they can answer their mothers' questions satisfactorily — they don't actually want to answer them for reasons already explained — but we do need to work to ensure they have the necessary range of words on hand when they need them.

There are two reasons, I think, why mothers aren't generally satisfied with the answer 'good'. The first is that they still see their son as the small boy who confided in them on a regular basis. The young man standing in front of them looks like their son, but suddenly he's not acting as he always has. This shutting down of communication is frightening to mothers. They've been aware, through the antics of other family members and via the media, that boys change as teenagers, but have never realised that their sons, too, would disappear behind the wall of adolescence. It's panic that drives them to go on interrogating their boys, panic they believe will be calmed only by acquiring more information.

The second reason mothers don't stop asking questions is because they're used to the flow of language. Women (and I include myself here) won't be satisfied with one word when ten would be better. As a gender we women love talking and when life presents a challenge, we respond by talking our way through it. We discuss problems with our colleagues, our best friend or friends, our doctor — and sometimes with anyone who will listen. In this way we find solutions and because that's our experience, we often assume that talking to our sons will calm the sense of panic we feel as our boys show they're approaching adolescence. On the basis of my own experience and the many conversations I've had with the mothers of boys, it seems we women convince ourselves that if we keep talking to our boys, all will be well. It makes no difference that the boys don't answer willingly; that just makes us all the more determined to keep asking the questions.

In contrast to mothers' reactions to the 'good' response, when I talked with principals and fathers there was general agreement among them that there are times when that is all boys need or want to say — and that the same can be said of adult men. Many men I spoke to, both parents and teachers, said they often felt that a single-word answer to a question was enough, though their wives and partners were completely unable to understand why.

'Do you ever talk about your feelings?'

'No, not really.'

'Why not?'

'Because talking about it just brings it all back up again. No point in that.'

In the wings of male prisons, I noticed again and again that, when a man's emotions, predominantly anger, were stirred and he couldn't find the words to articulate what he was feeling, he either shrugged and walked away or, if he was angry enough, used his fists. On a number of occasions I saw the same thing, albeit to a lesser degree, in the classrooms of boys' schools.

It stopped a long way short of fights breaking out, but I often saw students, annoyed by their inability to find a word or series of words to explain the idea in their head, eventually shrug and give up, retreating behind a monosyllabic answer and adding to an ever-present sense of frustration. On some occasions I saw them deflect that frustration by targeting another boy either verbally or physically, often doing substantial damage in the process.

As I watched a boy trying to articulate an idea in his head, and as I considered, increasingly, the vulnerability of boys, I found myself wondering how many young men end their own lives because they can't find the words to say what they want to the important people in their lives.

The gorgeous boys currently attending secondary schools are going to move out into a complex and constantly changing world. They'll be expected to deal with a wide range of situations and they're going to have to negotiate relationships with, among others, their partners, their children and their employers. If they're to develop the emotional confidence they need to cope well in the world they must have an adequate word bank.

One last issue remains to be discussed: homosexuality and the homophobia that was easily detectable in the schools I visited. I've spoken of the language of insult that appeared to operate within all the schools I visited, and that almost all of it featured words that referred to homosexuality in a derogatory way. Words such as 'gay', 'faggot', 'queer' and 'homo' were regularly used by the students when talking to and about each other and were a common feature of discussions on the school campuses.

Whenever I raised their use of this language with the students, they were quick to point out that they weren't actually accusing the boy they were talking to or about of being homosexual. They were seeking mainly to annoy and occasionally to wound someone, most often one of their own friends. When asked when they'd first begun using insulting language as a way of communicating with other boys, the usual reply was 'at intermediate' (the two years before high school). When I asked one group of students why they used language connected to homosexuality to insult, they replied because being gay 'is the worst thing you can be'. This sentiment was echoed on several other occasions.

To a certain degree it was possible to see why this particular language had gained such currency. The students attending all-boys' schools were often singled out for attack by those at neighbouring co-ed schools and their insults all focused on the issue of homosexuality — the assumption seemed to be that only boys who were gay would attend a single-sex school. Some students spoke of being taunted with chants about having flies on both sides of their trousers; others talked of being ribbed about attending school on 'homo hill'. But this language of insult is by no means confined to boys' schools. Rather, it appears to be a characteristic of current youth culture : it's very common to hear young people describe something negative as 'gay'.

I was intrigued that the students I was meeting were demonstrating such a high level of homophobia and spent some time talking with them about it. It was primarily a case of peer learning: he used it and got a laugh and everyone thinks he's cool, so I'll use it too. Most students seemed to have learnt it from their peers, but some had copied older siblings.

There were times during the project when I was left with the impression that the boys thought homosexuality was something they were at extreme risk of catching and that if they didn't keep moving, they would be tagged and become 'it'. The innate pragmatism of the boys appeared to contribute to their horror of the idea they might be gay: whenever the subject was raised, they seemed to focus solely on the physical aspect of homosexual relationships rather than considering any of the wider issues.

Why they were so afraid of homosexuality I'm not sure.

Perhaps an erection at an inappropriate moment in a changing room had left them wondering. In any event it was clear the little bit of knowledge they did have was a potentially dangerous thing, likely to send them off down a path of proving they weren't gay. They did this both by the active pursuit of girls and by displaying what they considered to be overtly macho behaviour, such as drinking to get drunk and driving cars too fast.

The host of assumptions behind boys' use of homophobic language needs to be challenged. On one level, such assumptions make the school environment an unsafe place for any student who might be uncertain about his sexual orientation (and I believe a great many are, even if only in a very temporary way). On another level, many of the students attending these schools will go on to work in prominent positions within their communities and, if unchallenged, will take these assumptions into the workplace with them.

There can be no denying that the homophobia being overtly displayed by adolescent boys has been influenced by the views of the adult men around them. Until men are willing to confront their own homophobia, and the reasons for it, we won't see any improvement in the behaviour and attitude of adolescent boys in this regard. I'm not asking men to condone homosexuality if it's something they struggle to understand and/or deal with themselves. I *am* asking that they show courage in identifying whatever personal bias they might have and that they don't expect their sons to take on the same prejudices before they've had a chance to form their own views.

In a recent newspaper article a New Zealand journalist used words that sum up very effectively the reality of adolescent boys — 'Young men by law, boys by nature'. That's indeed what they are. We have the challenge of finding the ideal balance between letting them grow towards their potential and keeping them safe when they're unable or unwilling to do that for themselves. It's a tough challenge and in many instances we'll continue to get it wrong. What we have to remember is that we can only do it, mothers and fathers, parents and step-parents, parents and teachers, if we hold hands. We can't do it alone.

These gorgeous boys are on their way to becoming good men. They will contribute much to the world that awaits them if we, the adults in their lives, do our job to the very best of our ability.

+ Men need and/or want to belong to something bigger than themselves, to see themselves as part of a whole.

+ Boys make a very definite distinction between the men they admire and those they actually want to be like. They need to know a man personally before they can decide whether he merits being described as a good man.

+ We should be looking for potential positive male role models, heroes, not in the public arena but among the men in our boys' lives — their grandfathers, uncles, older brothers, teachers and coaches and, most of all, their fathers.

+ Both single-sex and co-ed schools have opportunities within their structures to create positive rites of passage for boys.

✦ Emotional confidence is the ability for boys to ask and answer reflective questions; the ability to think about the world and their part in it; and the ability to find the language to describe how they see that world.

✦ Many boys lack a satisfactory word bank.

✦ Women convince themselves that if they keep talking to their boys, all will be well.

✦ How many young men end their own lives because they can't find the words to say what they want to the important people in their lives?

✦ Homosexuality is connected to insult because, for boys, being gay is 'the worst thing you can be'.

✦ Boys seemed to think that homosexuality is something they're at extreme risk of catching.

✦ Until men confront their own homophobia and the reasons for it, we won't see any improvement in boys' behaviour and attitude.

Characteristics of a Good Man

Trust
Loyalty
Humour

———

Laid-back
Motivated
Honest

———

Has dreams and goals
Hard-working
Generous

———

Compassionate
Humble
Self-reliant

———

Respected
Respect for others
Sets a good example

———

Able to persevere
Able to lead from the front
Acts with forgiveness

———

Has the strength to express
   his emotions
Principled — sticks up
   for what he believes in
Strong enough to know
   when to ask for help

—

Self-confident (will have a go)
Has the courage to be who he is
   (knows who he is)
Follows through
   on what he promised

—

Committed to belonging to
   something
Being part of something
Attending
Participating

—

Brings sense to a situation
Brings humour to a situation
Challenges convention

—

Confident
Carries his authority
Pursues his uniqueness

—

Humour, humour, humour
Capable of lasting relationships
A risk taker

Straight talker
Honest
Empathetic

Enjoys his own physicality
Controls his anger
Shows love

Listens
Expresses his feelings
Can slow down and
  enjoy his own company

Can laugh at himself

Can have fun without alcohol

Good men don't sulk.

A researcher and social commentator, Celia Lashlie worked for 15 years within the prison service, starting in December 1985 as the first woman to work as a prison officer in a male prison in New Zealand. Her final role within the service was as manager of Christchurch Women's Prison, a position she left in September 1999.

Celia, who has a degree in anthropology and Maori, is the mother of two adult children. She now works on a number of projects, all of which are linked to improving the lives of at-risk children and empowering families to find their own solutions to the challenges they face.

In September 2004, she completed the Good Man Project. The project, which facilitated discussion within and between 25 boys' schools throughout New Zealand, aimed to create a working definition of what makes a good man in the 21st century.

What arose from the project was a significant insight into the minds of teenage boys, and what they are feeling at this period in their lives. There are also some challenging suggestions for parents, as well as a call for women in particular to rethink the way they interact with the men in their lives — their sons and their husbands — if they want to see their sons become the good men they want them to be.

Celia Lashlie's first book, *The Journey to Prison: Who Goes and Why*, was a bestseller and critical success. This was followed by *He'll Be OK: Growing Gorgeous Boys into Good Men*, which has proved to be an enduring bestseller since its initial publication. This Australian edition is the book's second edition, and Celia continues to work on these and similar issues with schools and parents in both Australia and New Zealand.